WITHDRAWN

"Broke by the War"

BROKE BY THE WAR

Letters of a Slave Trader

Edited by Edmund L. Drago

University of South Carolina Press

Published in Columbia, South Carolina, by the
University of South Carolina Press
Manufactured in the United States of America

Library of Congress Cataloging-in-Publication Data

McElveen, A. J., d. 1874.
    Broke by the war : letters of a slave trader / edited by Edmund L.
Drago.
        p.   cm.
    Chiefly correspondence from A.J. McElveen to Ziba B. Oakes.
    Includes bibliographical references and index.
    ISBN 0-87249-763-1 (hard cover : acid-free)
    1. Slave traders — South Carolina — Charleston — Correspondence.
2. Slave-trade — South Carolina — Charleston — History — 19th century —
Sources. 3. Charleston (S.C.) — History — 1775-1865 — Sources.
4. McElveen, A. J., d. 1874 — Correspondence. 5. Oakes, Ziba B.,
1806-1871 — Correspondence. I. Oakes, Zib B., 1806-1871.
II. Title.
E442.M35   1991
975.7'915 — dc20   91-17887

To my wife, Cheryle

Contents

Acknowledgments

A variety of persons made this book possible. Margaretta Childs introduced me to the Oakes Papers. Harry M. Lightsey, Jr., President of the College of Charleston, provided financial support and release time. Laura Monti, Keeper of Rare Books and Manuscripts, Boston Public Library, was gracious. Her staff, especially Giuseppe Bisaccia, Eugene Zepp, Roberta Zonghi, and Mary Ann Katsiane, were extremely helpful. Moreover, these letters have been published by courtesy of the Trustees of the Boston Public Library.

Other individuals to whom I am grateful include Michael Finefrock, who helped me select an appropriate laptop computer to transcribe the letters. Jane Pease, William Pease, Clarence Walker, and Lacy Ford, Jr., read a draft of the manuscript. In my research, I benefited from the advice of Michael Les Benedict, Paul Finkelman, Mark Fowler, Kermit Hall, Richard Hill, John McKivigan, Todd Savitt, and John Winberry. Harry Johnson, Register of Mesne Conveyance, Sumter County, helped make my stay in Sumter a success. W. Esmonde Howell, First Vice President of the Sumter County Genealogical Society, provided important information about the genealogy of the McElveen family. William T. Milhomme, Reference Supervisor, Massachusetts Archives at Columbia Point, guided me to some important documents dealing with the Oakes-Christie family. Elizabeth Newsom, Curator, Waring Historical Library, Medical University of South Carolina, enlightened me on nineteenth-century medical terms. The staffs of the Rare Book and Manuscript Library, Columbia University, and the Baker Library,

---

Harvard University, were most cooperative. Dorothy Fludd, Sheila Seaman, and Michael Phillips, colleagues at the Robert Scott Small Library, College of Charleston, gave continual assistance. Finally, I want to thank Warren Slesinger, Acquisitions Manager, University of South Carolina Press, and Kenneth M. Stampp for their encouragement.

"Broke by the War"

Introduction

With the surrender of Charleston imminent on 17 February 1865, Northern journalists scrambled to reach the city. None was more enterprising than Charles Carleton Coffin, war correspondent for the Boston *Daily Journal*, whose nom de plume was "Carleton." On 17 February he secured passage on the steamer *Fulton*, which brought him to the federal blockading fleet. His account of the raising of the Stars and Stripes over Fort Sumter was the first to appear all over the country. General Quincy A. Gillmore invited Coffin to accompany him. Units of the Twenty-first United States Colored Troops traveled from Morris Island to a landing in Charleston harbor at the South Atlantic Wharf. Their commander accepted the surrender of Charleston. The portion of the city immediately occupied by federal troops was referred to as "Gillmore Town."[1]

With an eye for the spectacular, Coffin subsequently headed toward the downtown area where the slave brokers had their offices and slave marts. Acutely aware of the interests of his Northern readers, Coffin wanted to expose the inner workings of the slave trade. He and other journalists found their story in the vicinity of Chalmers and State streets. A mayor had wanted to contain a public eyesore and reduce covert abuse of the slaves. Although the city's efforts to limit slave auctions to a single public place failed, many of the brokers had offices or marts in that neighborhood. In a dispatch dated 24 February 1865, Coffin told his readers that the slave traders were not to be found in an "out-of-the-way" place. "The brokers in flesh and blood took good care to be well buttressed," he wrote. "They set up their mart in a respectable quarter, with St. Michael's and the guard house, the Registry of Deeds and the Sunday School Depository, the Court House and the Theological Library around them to uphold and sustain them, and make their calling respectable." Among the "score of men" dealing "in the bodies and souls of men" were T. Ryan and Son, M. McBride, J. S. Riggs, Jr., and Z. B. Oakes, whose offices were on State and Chalmers streets.[2]

It was on Chalmers Street that Coffin located "the Slave Mart — a building with a large iron gate in front above which in large gilt letters was the word MART." Opening the iron gate, he entered a hall about sixty feet long and twenty feet wide with a long table running the length of the hall. At the end was a door opening into a yard. With the help of a freedman, he forced the locked door open, and saw "a four story brick building, with grated windows and iron doors — a prison." Coffin continued, "The yard is walled by high buildings. He who entered there left all hope behind. A small room adjoining the hall was the place where women were subjected to the lascivious gaze of brutal men. There were the steps, up which thousands of men, women and children have walked to their places on the table, to be knocked off to the highest bidder." The complex Coffin described was known as Ryan's Mart, or the Mart in Chalmers Street. The hall he entered, erected by the broker Z. B. Oakes, would become Charleston's Old Slave Mart Museum.[3]

While rummaging through the mart, it occurred to Coffin that perhaps William Lloyd Garrison, Wendell Phillips, or even Massachusetts governor John A. Andrew "would like to make a speech from those [very] steps" climbed by the slaves to the auction table. Trophies included the gilt star of the mart and the great lock from the outer gate. "The steps and locks are on their way to Boston," Coffin told his readers. "The key of the French Bastil[l]e hangs at Mt. Vernon." Much like modern Berliners tearing off pieces of the Berlin Wall in 1989, Northerners wanted to send home hard evidence of the oppressors' inhumanity.[4]

On the evening of 9 March 1865, a large audience gathered at Boston's Music Hall to listen to Charles Coffin as he presented the steps to the Ward Eleven Freedmen's Aid Society. The journalist read from "a scrapbook found by him in a broker's office in Charleston," which included bills of sale of women and children, advertisements of sales, and letter books. Although Governor Andrew "was unable to be present," a thunder of applause greeted William Lloyd Garrison as he mounted the slave steps. A communication from John G. Whittier best expressed the sentiment of the group: "Let these infernal hieroglyphics and symbols of the worship of Anti-Christ be carefully preserved. Lay them side by side with the racks of the Inquisition and the keys of the Bastille. Let them tell the generations to come of that most hideous form of human depravity."[5]

Despite the impression his February dispatch created, Coffin did not act alone, but rather was one of several reporters pillaging the "HEATHEN TEMPLES AND OTHER RELICS OF BARBARISM." He was accompanied by "Berwick," a correspondent for the New York *Daily Tribune*. "Berwick" was none other than James Redpath, staunch abolitionist and biographer of John Brown. "We visited all the slave pens, and broke them open," Redpath reported. "What a tale of wickedness, these letter books do tell! We carried off, among us all, the entire correspondence of these establishments, the bell, the auctioneer's block, the locks, and one sign."[6]

On 20 February 1865 Redpath took some 652 business letters of Z. B. Oakes from "a slave pen," probably the slave mart, or Oakes's office at 7 State Street (as the addresses on the letters suggest). Those letters Redpath failed to scoop up were taken by Coffin. The next day Redpath greeted a young

officer marching into Charleston with the Fifty-fifth Massachusetts Regiment, singing John Brown's song. The lieutenant
turned out to be George Thompson Garrison, the eldest son
of the noted abolitionist. Perhaps this chance meeting and
following events inspired Redpath to turn the Oakes correspondence over to the family patriarch. With the media and
posterity in mind, Secretary of War Edwin M. Stanton invited
the press, William Lloyd Garrison, and other anti-slavery celeb-
rities to a flag-raising ceremony at Fort Sumter on 14 April
1865. The event was to commemorate the fourth anniversary
of Fort Sumter's surrender under Union Major Robert Anderson to the Confederacy. Garrison and some eighty other digni-
taries sailed from New York to South Carolina aboard the
steamer *Arago*. The ceremony was presided over by Major
General Anderson. The main oration was given by Henry
Ward Beecher. Garrison was accompanied by his son George,
who had received a furlough from Stanton for that purpose.
Redpath had this opportunity and others to present the letters
to Garrison during his three-day visit in Charleston. The most
likely occasion, however, was on the day of departure at the
wharf where Garrison was given an emotional farewell presided
over by Redpath. The party continued on its journey to Florida
but shortly thereafter received the news of Lincoln's assassina-
tion. Perhaps the sudden return North and the ensuing havoc
caused Garrison to forget to mention the letters in his writings.[7]

The Oakes letters remained in the family until Garrison's
sons, Wendell Phillips Garrison and Francis Jackson Garrison,
completed a biography of their father. In April 1891 the family
turned over the Garrison papers to the Boston Public Library.
The secretary of the Board of Trustees reported a gift to the
library of "certain original letters and manuscripts belonging
to William Lloyd Garrison which served as the foundation for
the biography of him written by his sons." On 11 November
1891 Francis Jackson Garrison also donated the Oakes letters.

They were not organized chronologically and remain today in the order in which they were received. There are a calendar and index which document how Redpath discovered and turned them over to the family patriarch.[8]

ZIBA B. OAKES, CHARLESTON BROKER AND AUCTIONEER

The Oakes family plot is located in Charleston's Magnolia Cemetery. There is a certain irony that the Oakes Papers ended up in New England. Ziba himself was born in Sangersville, Maine, in 1806, the son of Samuel Oakes and Mary (Polly) Burrill Oakes. His wife Margaret Garaux Christie was born in Boston in 1813, the daughter of John Christie, a mariner, and Rachel Oakes Christie. The Christie and Oakes families, living at various times in Boston and parts of Maine, were closely related. When John Christie died in 1816, Samuel Oakes was appointed an appraiser of his estate.[9]

In 1817 Samuel Oakes brought his family to Charleston, where Ziba later attended the school of John England, the Catholic bishop. His father entered various business enterprises—first, a grocery store at Gadsden's Wharf (1819-1822), then a sugar store at 53 Queen Street (1829), and finally a store at the corner of Market and Church streets. Young Oakes would eventually become involved. The 1831 city directory described the family establishment as "Oakes S & Son sugar store." That same year he married Margaret, who might have been a cousin. By the 1850s Z. B. Oakes was a broker and auctioneer with an office at 7 State Street. Credit reports for the R.G. Dun & Co. described him as an extremely capable and successful businessman. After the war he was a "Real Estate Broker" and insurance agent, "representing several influential companies." He served the city as an alderman (1865-1868), and commissioner of the Markets and Alms House.[10]

Men such as Oakes shared a commercial ethos and networking system that encouraged them not to leave the business to become gentlemen farmers after they had attained wealth and become pillars of the community. When Oakes died on 25 May 1871, his passing was front-page news in the Charleston *Daily Courier*. A number of organizations invited their members to attend the funeral of their distinguished friend at his residence on Meeting and Hudson streets: Charleston Board of Trade; Landmark Lodge, No. 76, A.F.M.; Fellowship Society; South Carolina Commandery, No. 1, Knights Templar (Oakes was Generalissimo); and I.O.O.F. (Odd Fellows) South Carolina Lodge No. 1 (Oakes was treasurer for several years). The Charleston broker had also been an officer in the Ancient Free Masons of South Carolina. At the time of his death, he was still active in business, serving on the Board of Underwriters. The Unitarians did not doubt that their former vestryman had earned his eternal reward. The day after his funeral, their minister R. P. Cutler delivered a discourse, "Immortality, and the Recognition of Friends in Heaven."[11]

SCOPE OF THE OAKES PAPERS

Nearly all of the 652 letters in the collection were addressed to Z. B. Oakes or his company. None was written by Oakes himself. Some letters came from major slave-trading centers outside the state: Montgomery (21), Richmond (10), and New Orleans (8). The vast majority, however, were from cities and towns in South Carolina or Georgia: Sumterville, including Sumter, Sumter Court House, Sumter District (125); Savannah (118); Charleston (42); Augusta (34); Summerville, S.C. (17); Goulding, S.C. (15); Hamburg, S.C. (14); and Aiken, S.C. (11). About 529 letters, or 81.1 percent, came from South Carolina (350, or 53.7 percent) and Georgia (179, or 27.4 percent). The brokers, agents, and other clients most frequently mentioned in the index to the Oakes Papers were: A. J. McElveen, Sumterville, 131; William Wright, Savannah, 58; Wylly and Montmollin, Savannah, 24; Thomas Limehouse, Goulding and Summerville, 23; Burch Kirkland and Company, Montgomery, 13; R. M. Owings and Company, Hamburg, 11; Scranton Johnson and Company, Savannah, 11; and Leighton and Sherman, Georgetown, S.C., 10.[12]

THE OAKES PAPERS AND THE LITERATURE ON THE DOMESTIC SLAVE TRADE

For nearly sixty years Frederic Bancroft's *Slave-Trading in the Old South* has remained the classic work on the internal slave trade in the United States. Written from a pro-abolitionist perspective, the book covered the domestic slave trade from its earliest beginnings in the eighteenth century until the Civil War. The domestic trade grew dramatically after the international slave trade was closed in 1808. Bancroft's study concentrated on the major urban slave-trading centers: the District of Columbia, Richmond, Memphis, New Orleans, Savannah, and Charleston. Bancroft's chapter on Charleston, rich in texture, benefited from the half-dozen trips the scholar had made to the city and the interviews and correspondence he had had with the descendants of Low Country planters.[13]

Michael Tadman's *Speculators and Slaves* expanded Bancroft's earlier efforts. Using sophisticated quantification unknown to Bancroft's generation, Tadman demonstrated that for each decade between 1820 and 1860 about 200,000 slaves left the Upper South; most of them, perhaps 60 to 70 percent, moved as a result of the slave trade rather than planter migration. The result was devastating in terms of the division of black families. According to Tadman, "over half of all slaves who fell into the hands of the slave trader would either have been forcibl[y] separated from a spouse or have been children who were forcibly separated from one or both of their parents."[14]

Using the Oakes Papers, Tadman demonstrated that the slave trade in South Carolina went far beyond Charleston. While Bancroft described only three traders outside of Charleston in the 1850s, Tadman identified sixty-five. More importantly, the Oakes letters allowed him to document the mentalities of masters, slave traders, and the slaves themselves. The slave traders, in their own words, were hard-headed businessmen pursuing profits according to well-established practices. The wealthier ones were pillars of their communities, while the less wealthy saw the trade as an honest calling to support their families.[15]

Perusing this collection of letters, the reader may feel the tension created by their depersonalizing business tone in contrast to the human situation of the slaves themselves. "A negro woman in this place has been to us," a Georgetown client writes to Oakes, "and says a son of hers by name of Boston is now in the work house in Charleston for sale and that he wishes to come and work in our mills. . . . Will you please ascertain whether it is so and what the fellows habits are and best terms on which he can be purchased & oblige." Sometimes the feelings of the slaves break through these letters, especially in their efforts to run away and retain family ties. The impact of a separation is poignantly captured in a message from a wife to her husband, recently sold: "I never expect to see you again. . . . I am very much distressed now at being separated from you. Remember me and I will think of you. Write to me after you are settled." The pathos of this message had little effect on the master, who was pleased with the business transaction. According to Tadman, "the racism of most masters was so profound that they saw black families as ephemeral concerns and blacks' emotions and thoughts as infantile or even bestial, and thus found it easy to regard themselves as paternalists."[16]

The Oakes correspondence also suggests that the internal slave trade, evolving from an entrepreneurial base, became a force for modernizing South Carolina. Men such as Z. B. Oakes and J. S. Riggs, Jr., two of Charleston's wealthier men in 1860, were salesmen following in their parents' footsteps. They did not come from established planter families like fellow brokers Louis DeSaussure and Thomas N. Gadsden. Their careers showed how adaptive entrepreneurial capitalism was. The two family patriarchs, Samuel Oakes and John S. Riggs, Sr., came to South Carolina as commercial-minded men determined to make their way by finding a need and supplying it. Samuel Oakes was a grocer, while J. S. Riggs, Sr., was a saddler and harness maker. Their sons became brokers and auctioneers, selling almost everything, including real estate, schooners, horses, and slaves.[17]

Ironically, in a pre-modern South, the slave brokers could be considered among the earliest proponents of a "New South." As men on the make, they were extremely attuned to fluctuations in the marketplace, both regional and national. They saw that railroads and banks were vital to their region's prosperity as well as to their own success. For Oakes and Riggs, the railroads opened up new ways to carry on and expand their trade. Slaves, once moved by "coffles" (gangs on foot), could now be more efficiently transported by railroad. The term "coffle" is seldom mentioned in the Oakes letters. Business correspondence, especially about market prices, could be sent more quickly by railroad. Mail was even occasionally carried "By Servants *on S. Co R R.*" When bloodhounds were needed to hunt down runaway slaves, they could be sent to the area by railroad. The railroads were also valuable in shipping foodstuffs, a boon to Upcountry farmers and Charleston grocers. Every day except Sunday, "the Night Passenger and Freight Express Trains," the Charleston *Mercury* announced in 1853, "will take light freight and perishable articles up, and Poultry, Eggs, Fruit, and other light articles down, to and from the following Stations, viz: Summerville, Ridgeville, Branchville, Lowry's, Graham's, Blackville, Williston, Aiken and Graniteville on the Hamburg Branch, and for Orangeburg, Lewisville, Fort Motte and Gadsden on the Columbia Road."[18]

Sumter District, like other markets, could be more fully exploited after the arrival of the railroad in 1848. The railroad reached Sumterville in 1852. By the 1850s Z. B. Oakes had set up an office in the town of Sumterville (later renamed Sumter) and had employed A. J. McElveen as his agent in the area, which also included Darlington District. Besides purchasing slaves for Oakes to sell, McElveen supplied him information on railroad stocks, bonds, real estate, and other investment opportunities. The value of a plantation "finely adapted" to growing cotton was significantly increased by its proximity to a railroad. An advertisement selling an eleven-hundred-acre tract in the Sumter area boasted, "It is remarkable for its healthiness near to the Railroad, and convenient to Church, and is very desirably situated in a community proverbial for its morality."[19]

The Oakes Papers cover the boom times of the 1850s, when cotton profits and the arrival of railroads dramatically impacted South Carolina districts, especially those in the Upcountry. As Lacy Ford wrote, "men with an eye for the main chance opened new stores both to make a fast buck from the business generated by railroad construction and in anticipation of the increase in commercial activity that would follow." In 1853 goods sold in the Upcountry were worth $2,717,776, but six years later, the total value reached over four million dollars.[20]

The expanding slave trade resulted in additional business for doctors and lawyers. Doctors appear regularly in the Oakes correspondence. They were required to issue certificates on the soundness of the slaves being sold. Sometimes this led to sticky situations and the threat of a messy lawsuit, especially when it involved the ability of a slave woman to have children. In April 1854 T. L. Gelzer of Summerville told Oakes that Dulcina, purchased the previous December, "has been proven unsound. She has been affected with a uterine disease for several years & has been pronounced incurable by the

Physician who attended her previous to her being brought to Charleston for Sale." But the physician in question, J. B. Witherspoon, subsequently explained to Oakes: "I know many females who have [Dysmenorrhea?] badly, who are yet sound and are considered in good health, and except for a few days at their Menstrual periods are as healthy as others." Witherspoon was a member of the South Carolina Medical Association and an officer in "The District Medical Society of Sumter and Clarendon."[21]

When the war ended, men like Oakes and Riggs continued to prosper. With their real estate holdings intact and their ability to sell undiminished, they survived the war in grand style. During Presidential Reconstruction, Oakes served as a city alderman. Unable to sell slaves, the Charleston broker went into the general insurance business, with an office at 4 Broad Street (a more prestigious location than 7 State Street). He became the agent for Queen Fire Insurance Company, of Liverpool and London; Home Fire Insurance Company, 135 Broadway, New York; and Astor Fire Insurance Company, 16 Wall Street, New York. An investigator for R.G. Dun & Co. wrote in 1868 that Oakes "saved money out of the war." From 1860 to 1865 he had been a director of Southwestern Railroad Bank. Now agent for a New York insurance company, the broker was "worthy of all confidence." John S. Riggs, Jr., remained a real estate broker after the war, amassed a considerable fortune, and became president of the City Railway Company. When he died in February 1899, the Charleston *Daily News and Courier* did not mention his career as a slave broker but described him as "one of the city's pioneers in progress" and "a self-made man in every sense of the word."[22]

As agents of modernization before the war, these men were probably better able to adapt to the new order of things than some traditional-minded planters. Trained as salesmen, they sold insurance rather than human beings after the war. Some of them were more sympathetic to the education of blacks than many of their conservative neighbors. In 1866 black educator Francis L. Cardozo, in charge of the New York-based American Missionary Association efforts in Charleston, needed to find land for his new school (later named Avery Normal Institute); he consulted J. S. Ryan, a former "slave-Broker, as well as a Broker of Real Estate," who was "said to be worth half a million." Cardozo reported that Ryan offered "Five Hundred dollars towards the erection of our school provided he has the right of sending two colored scholars, and he offered to collect Five Hundred more from his friends — the Brokers." Ryan's motives might not have been completely altruistic. He had fathered several children by a black mistress he was living with in 1865.

Ironically, it was the son of slave broker John S. Riggs who first suggested restoring Charleston's Old Slave Mart. "As we are able to take care of TOURISTS next season, I am thinking of putting the Old Slave Mart in such shape that visitors would be able to get some kind of idea of how it looked in former days," Sidney S. Riggs wrote to Frederic Bancroft in 1924. "I would welcome any suggestions from you as to this."[23]

THE McELVEEN LETTERS AND A CHANGING SUMTER

The letters from A. J. McElveen of Sumterville (Sumter) to Z. B. Oakes of Charleston total 135, the largest number from any single trader in the collection. Six additional letters relating to McElveen bring the total to 141, or roughly 22 percent of the Oakes correspondence. These 141 letters cover the boom years from 1852 up through the panic of 1857: 1852 (1), 1853 (26), 1854 (59), 1855 (15), 1856 (23), 1857 (17). There are gaps. After an initial letter from McElveen in January 1852, there are no letters until July 1853. Likewise, there is a sixteen-month hiatus between 8 March 1855 and 8 July 1856. As noted above, those Oakes letters James Redpath did not scoop up were carried off by Charles Coffin. The letters taken by Coffin may account for some of these gaps. The 1866 edition of his *Four Years of Fighting* had excerpts from letters addressed to Z. B. Oakes, two written by A. J. McElveen. These two excerpts did not come from the McElveen letters in the Oakes Papers deposited in the Boston Public Library.[24]

Despite these gaps, the McElveen letters in the Boston collection document the Sumter slave trade and its connection with Charleston. Most of the 141 letters (121, or 85.8 percent) were addressed from the Sumter area: Sumterville (86); Sumter Court House (25); Sumter (5); Sumter District (3); Mayesville (1); and Sandy Grove (1). Uniting three counties formerly part of Camden District (i.e., Claremont, Clarendon, and Salem), Sumter District was established in 1800. Originally measuring 1,672 square miles, it was reduced to 681 square miles after Clarendon and Lee separated from it in 1855 and 1902, respectively. Its judicial center, the courthouse, was located in the small town of Sumterville. In 1855 the town was renamed Sumter, and in 1868 Sumter District became Sumter County. After the invention of the cotton gin, the cotton culture spread rapidly into the area. The number of slaves increased dramatically. A predominantly white populated area in 1790, Sumter District was overwhelmingly black by 1860. Although the number of whites multiplied, their percentage of the total population declined as follows: 60.9 percent (1790); 47.6 percent (1800); 28.7 percent (1860).[25]

As the total population grew, Thomas Sumter, for whom the district was named, championed greater representation in the South Carolina legislature for those living in the upper portion of the state. After the Compromise of 1808, the power of the Upcountry increased as its white population and wealth augmented. However, the Low Country, with the support of black-majority districts, maintained its control of the Senate. Although the Upcountry came to be defined as "the thirteen election districts lying north and west of the fall line," Sumter District, along with Darlington, was considered part of the state's original "Upper Division." The McElveen letters reveal the retention of a backcountry mentality despite economic and demographic changes.[26]

THE McELVEENS OF PUDDING SWAMP

The milieu that produced A. J. McElveen was shaped by a backcountry mentality, the American Revolution, and a Scotch-Irish heritage. The McElveen clan of Sumter District, whose ancestors probably first settled the Williamsburg region, was Scotch-Irish. The late genealogist Margaret McElveen said she could trace the McElveens to the Pudding Swamp area of Black River but not to where they came from in the old country. According to legend, Pudding Swamp got its name "for the blood and liver puddings made there at 'hog-killing' time."

Like most of the early European pioneers of the South Carolina backcountry, the Scotch-Irish located themselves along major waterways such as Black River. These waterways and their tributaries provided both a means of subsistence and transportation with an outlet to the Atlantic. Towns, farms, and plantations grew up around them. Black River (called Wee Nee by the Indians) formed a large network of streams (sometimes called rivers) in the area between Lynches Creek and Wateree River. Corn grew in abundance; the "rivers and swamps [of Black River] swarmed with enormous quantities of excellent edible fish and the forests were full of herds of deer. Wild turkeys were abundant." During the American Revolution, Charles Lord Cornwallis allegedly remarked, "Williamsburg is worth capturing for the fish in Black River."[27]

Two large streams, Douglas Swamp and Hope Swamp, formed Pudding Swamp, which flowed into Black River below the Williamsburg County line. "The people who first settled the area about Douglas Swamp, Mount Hope Swamp, and Pudding Swamp, were mostly the Scotch-Irish which spread-over from the Williamsburg settlement," Sumter County historian Janie Revill noted. "Their names were Frierson, Witherspoon, Bradley, Wilson, McBride, Gordon, McElveen, and McFadden." However appealing the new settlers might have found the swamplands, Northern travelers were not so appreciative. "South Carolina, at least the region traversed by railway, is the most miserable country I ever saw," Lyman Abbott declared in 1856. "Swamp, swamp, swamp, all day long. No villages, no houses, no inhabitants, no green fields, nothing but an interminable swamp. Every half-hour we stop in the middle of the swamp." As late as 1922, more than a quarter of the acreage in Sumter County was still considered swamp land.[28]

The McElveen family patriarch might have been Adam McElveen, who in 1760 received a land grant in Salem County, later to become Sumter District. By 1770 the McElveen name was closely linked with the Pudding Swamp area. The Pudding Swamp settlement of Muckelveeny (also spelled "Mackelveeny") probably referred to Adam McElveen's holdings. His sons appear to have been John and William McElveen. William McElveen, Sr., was born in Sumter District on 10 May 1757. During the American Revolution he served in the South Carolina militia as a private. Although he was illiterate, he managed to obtain a respectable amount of land, much of it through bounties. In 1804 he received state land grants totaling nearly twelve hundred acres. The bulk of the land was located "in Salem County on the North Side of Black River & West Side of Pudding Swamp on a Fork of John Creek a Water Branch of Black River." The area today is part of Clarendon County, which separated from Sumter District in 1855. William McElveen, Sr., apparently was a member of Midway Presbyterian Church, founded in 1802 by settlers from Williamsburg. The church, located on the northeastern branch of Black River in present-day Clarendon County, was halfway between Sumter

District's Salem Black River Church and the Williamsburg Presbyterian Church.[29]

William McElveen, Sr., came to adulthood before the cotton gin had turned Sumter District into primarily a cotton-producing area. The intestate proceedings initiated after his death on 8 April 1837 suggest that the eighty-year-old man was representative of the early settlers, who had made their living raising livestock and growing corn. His estate, worth less than two thousand dollars, included nearly eleven hundred acres of land and two slaves. In addition to a single lot of cotton, McElveen possessed one lot of corn, nine head of cattle, twenty hogs, thirteen geese, ten fowl, and a spinning wheel. In 1838 the land appraised at $1,098 was sold for $436. McElveen's widow Rhoda (Rhody) received a third of the proceeds. The rest was divided equally among numerous other relatives, including Andrew J. McElveen, probably the author of the McElveen letters.[30]

Born during the War of 1812, A. J. McElveen might have been named after Andrew Jackson, another Scotch-Irishman, who is still very much a part of Sumter County's collective image of itself. Absent from antebellum manuscript census records, A. J. is an elusive figure. Although during the 1850s he transacted mortgages involving slaves, there is no record of his owning independently any real estate in Sumter District before the Civil War. The Oakes Papers offer precious little about A. J.'s background, where he lived, or who his relatives were. The Sumter District slave trader maintained an office in Sumterville and resided on a place not too distant from the town. He mentioned a brother, nephews, and "little Oakes," a son born on 9 July 1856.

Nine months earlier, on 29 September 1855, one Andrew J. McElveen entered into a marriage settlement with Frances Hodge Mellett, the widow of Dr. James L. Mellett (1814-1853). She had received a third of her late husband's estate; her two children, the other two-thirds. As a professional slave trader, A. J. was well acquainted with most Sumter District doctors. He was in a fortuitous position to help the grieving widow, who needed to sell her late husband's slaves. The estate was "considerably in debt." The Mellett and Hodge families, perhaps fearful of a too hasty remarriage and desirous of protecting the financial assets of the widow, might have urged Frances to seek the marriage settlement. The portion of the Mellett estate "allotted and set apart as her portion therein to the sole and separate use of the said Frances H. Mellett for and during her natural life [was] to be in no manner liable for the debts liabilities assignments or transfer of the said Andrew J. McElveen or any future husband." A. J. probably also wanted to shield Frances from any debts he incurred in his rather risky business.[31]

AN ITINERANT SLAVE TRADER

Slave trading offered an opportunity for real economic advancement. Nathan Bedford Forrest and Isaac Franklin used the trade to become powerful commission merchants and wealthy planters. Major slave brokers established permanent businesses in cities such as New Orleans and Charleston. A host of itinerant slave traders served them and tried to emulate their success. The McElveen letters, written by an agent to his boss, offer insight into their world.[32]

Though these letters were shaped by the wishes of a demanding and tough-minded boss whose presence is always felt, McElveen's respect and admiration for Oakes appear genuine. The Charleston broker was for his agent a role model as a family man as well as a businessman. McElveen admired Oakes's family life. His business letters became a vehicle for him to court Susan, a close friend of the family, perhaps a relative of Mrs. Oakes (whom she accompanied to Boston). McElveen's affection for Susan advanced from "do let me here from Susan" in

October 1853 to "Send my love to Susan" in May 1854. Two months later he pleaded to his employer: "Please tell Mrs oakes to tell Susan I hope She is not fagot me & tell her I think more a bout her Since She has bin absent than I Ever did   tell Susan to Send me her Degarotype." Susan never returned McElveen's affections, and in October 1855, McElveen married the widow Frances Hodge Mellett.[33]

Although McElveen admired Oakes, he also exhibited a back-country mentality. Even during the boom times of the 1850s, attachment to the old ways (sneeringly referred to as "Old Fogyism" by the apostles of progress) remained an obstacle to changes being wrought by railroads and banks. In Charleston on 8 February 1853 the Methodist minister Whiteford Smith presented a petition to the annual meeting of stockholders of the South Carolina Railroad Company and Southwestern Railroad Bank. He had been appointed by disgruntled stockholders who had met at "a meeting of the South Carolina Conference" in Sumterville the previous month. The minister and his friends decried "the desecration of the Lord's day, by the operations of the Company." The company agreed to discontinue all Sunday labor "except as regards the carrying of public Mail, and other cases of emergency." Some stockholders complained bitterly that "a Methodist Conference bought stock in the South-Carolina Railroad Company, for the sole purpose of intermeddling." In 1854 a Sumterville newspaper decried a "speedy repair" on the Sabbath as a "deliberate desecration."[34]

For McElveen life was a constant struggle with evil. "I am in Some trouble for Several days past," he told Oakes in October 1853. "One of my nephews got Shot dead Some ten days a go, Simpley from Keeping company with bad men." After Charleston suffered through a particularly bad bout of yellow fever, McElveen told Oakes, "I am fearful these judgements are Sent on the place for the wicked Evils of the people." Perhaps out of deference to Oakes's feelings, he added, "However I will drop that we are wicked in the country."[35]

McElveen's lot in life was hard. His job was primarily to purchase slaves in the Sumter-Darlington area for Oakes. He was occasionally helped by his brother. Although he traveled by horse, he often used the railroads. Frequently absent from home for days, he found life on the road grinding. "The night train broke down a bout Eleven o clock the Evening I left," he reported to Oakes in February 1855. "Consequentely I was detaind until the morning train came up to Kingsville. no passengers was hurt but I had the Coldest Ride up that night I Ever had I think." McElveen had to worry about getting the slaves to Charleston. "I am Glad to here you have men wating for Stock," he reported in 1853. "I hope to get themdown Safe . . . [but] the R.R. is Broken down and I am fearful It will be trobled to Get them down Safe." The ingenious and repeated efforts of the slaves to run away or avoid being sold drained McElveen. "Mr Oakes James is cutting up," he wrote in exasperation in 1856. "I could Sell him like hot cakes if he would talk right. . . . the Boy is trying to make himself *unsound.*" Despite these problems and tensions, McElveen usually refrained from using physical violence, except as a last resort.[36]

Oakes and McElveen were probably less overtly cruel than most traders. Oakes was considered by some colleagues as too sensitive and too eager "to please negroes." McElveen, describing a skilled craftsman he bought, conceded the man was "Smarter" than he. Not once in his correspondence did McElveen ever use the term "slave." Both Oakes and McElveen, however, were in the business for profit. McElveen approached his job in a relatively dispassionate, dollars-and-cents way. He proclaimed one male slave as the "Best Stripped [naked] fellow I Ever Examined." Having purchased a slave with a missing toe, he apologized, "I could not Get one dollar nocked off for that," adding, "I dont think it Should lessen his value." Employing the jargon of the trade, he described slaves in a group as "head" and those of inferior quality as "scrubs." The routine way in which McElveen handled the tensions of his business is exemplified by his account of a deal in which he purchased a woman and daughter but failed to buy the man. "The woman will complain but She is unwilling to leave," McElveen warned Oakes. "I think She will need correcting.   I could not buy her husband   do try and Get $1300 for the woman & daughter."[37]

The greatest pressure on McElveen was finding high-quality "stock" at prices that would allow Oakes to resell at a profit. "The fact is," he wrote in 1853, "I cant find negros for Sale that will pay a profit." Ten months later he lamented, "I cant buy negros up here at the prices you Gave me." Facing stiff competition from western traders, McElveen decided to take a group of slaves to Alabama, but once there, he found the "trade not very Brisk."[38]

In a world of sharpies, McElveen struggled to retain his integrity and honor. He placed a high premium on keeping his word, something "honerable" men were expected to do. "I hope Mr McKay will not think for a moment I wished to cheat him   I never wish to deceive any man," he once pleaded. Another time he explained, "I dont deceive no man if I a[m] awise of the fact." Unfortunately, few men McElveen dealt with in the trade approached his standards. "It is Strange," he noted, "it is but the fewest number of men can be depended on in our day." The trader despised those colleagues who were dishonorable in their business practices. He described H. G. Burkett as "one of the poriest a pologes for a man I Ever Saw.   you can Judge no dependence attall in him."[39]

Ironically, McElveen's sense of honor and loyalty almost "Ruined" him financially and nearly landed him in jail. "I am astonished to think how I am deceived by men who promised to Give me there names on the Bonds and have backed out," he wrote on 21 February 1857. On 7 March he asked Oakes, "Give me advice   I have only one fortnight that is two weeks of Grace on my note   must I Suffer to be Sued or not." Two weeks later, he had resigned himself to losing the case and going to jail.[40]

Although A. J. McElveen survived this personal financial crisis and the nationwide recession of 1857, he never really prospered. Success was always elusive, usually somewhere else in "the West." Despite years of effort, often on the road away from his family, McElveen remained economically marginal. He failed to accumulate much real estate. In 1860 an agent for R.G. Dun & Co. reported that McElveen "purchases negroes in speculation, also plants, do not think he owns any property in his own right." Probably his age (forty-eight in 1861) and his occupation initially kept him from service in the Confederate Army. On 13 March 1863, the Darlington *Southerner* ran the advertisement: "FIFTY young and likely negroes — for which the highest cash price will be paid . . . A. J. McELVEEN, Sumter, S.C." On 1 August 1863 he enlisted as a private in Company I, Fourth Regiment, South Carolina State Troops, which was designed for "State service and local defense." This particular unit was formed from Captain Francis Marion Mellett's Company, Twentieth Regiment, South Carolina Militia. The captain was a relative of Mrs. McElveen's first husband. McElveen's six-month term ended on 1 February 1864. He reenlisted as a corporal on 16 April 1864, in the Fifth Battalion, South Carolina Reserves. Also known as Brown's Battalion, it went into service about 15 September 1864, and was stationed at the military prison in Florence, South Carolina. Corporal McElveen appeared on his company's muster roll from 15 September to 31 October 1864. The last entry on his personal records, dated 1864, was "Absent without leave."[41]

After the war an A. J. McElveen appeared as a small farmer, struggling to make a living in Privateer Township. Like many whites adjusting to the new order of things, he found himself competing with former slaves, some of whom he had bought or sold. His experience might explain why so many white farmers bitterly opposed Radical Reconstruction. Bankrupt by 1869, McElveen pledged his gold watch and "entire crop" as collateral for $150 worth of supplies at an interest rate of 25 percent. Whatever his politics, he entered into this agreement with the Republican George W. Reardon, an Irish stonecutter from Massachusetts, who had come to South Carolina before the war to work on the State House. The next year McElveen again pledged his "entire crop," for $150 in cash at the same interest rate. In 1871 the credit records of R.G. Dun & Co. described McElveen as "Broke by the war — old man." When he died in 1874, his estate was insolvent.[42]

Exactly who were A. J. McElveen's offspring, and what happened to them, especially "little Oakes," are questions impossible to answer with any certainty. According to the letters, "little Oakes" was born in 1856, making him fourteen in 1870. The 1870 census for Privateer Township listed a William McElveen, age fourteen, in the household of A. J. McElveen. In 1892 Jefferson Davis McElveen and William F. O. McElveen, described as the children of A. J. McElveen, contested the ownership of 169 acres in Privateer Township (possibly part of Frances McElveen's estate). Perhaps William F. O. McElveen was "little Oakes."[43]

EDITORIAL PROCEDURE

To reproduce as accurately as possible the McElveen letters, I relied on the guidelines formulated by Ira Berlin and his associates in their Freedmen and Southern Society Project. They preserved a sense of immediacy and intensely felt emotions. I hope that this method provides a similar insight into the world of an itinerant South Carolina slave trader.[44]

I made the following overt minor interventions:

————————

1. Annotating the text in notes to give the reader necessary background material.
2. Deleting salutations, closings, date and place lines; rewording this data to introduce each letter; and making postscripts as uniform as possible. The Oakes Papers are cataloged as Ms. Am. 322 at the Boston Public Library. In addition, every letter has an identifying number based on the order in which the papers were received. In parentheses at the end of each introduction of the letters is this numerical identification.
3. Using brackets to clarify those portions of the text that are partially illegible. Conjectures are accompanied by a question mark, e.g. [argued?]. Empty brackets, [   ], indicate a totally unintelligible word, or a missing word I cannot infer. Empty brackets with a note indicate that more than one word is missing or unintelligible. In the note I attempt to explain the number of unintelligible words or the extent of the missing passage.
4. Inserting into the text with curly brackets, {   }, material written in the margins or between lines.

The rest of the interventions were made without notation:
1. Eliminating inadvertent reduplication of words, and scratched out or canceled words (unless they added some meaning).
2. Omitting blank pages, or parts of blank pages.
3. Omitting addresses on the letters, usually on the back of the letter.
4. Deleting extraneous pen and pencil marks.
5. Bringing superscripts on line.

Although I attempted to preserve faithfully the punctuation and capitalization found in the letters, this sometimes proved difficult. Written in haste, periods and commas appeared as dashes. It was often impossible to distinguish a period from a comma, or an uppercase from a lowercase letter. In such instances, I usually followed modern usage. When an uppercase letter was used occasionally within a word, I made it lowercase. As an example, I changed "WhiteSide" to "Whiteside." Monetary and other numerical notations were made consistent. When eight hundred dollars was written as $8.00, or one hundred sixty-five pounds as 1.65 lbs, I deleted the period. I had to render into modern punctuation unconventional punctuation marks, especially at the ends of sentences. As already stated, commas and dashes could frequently be perceived as periods and vice versa. When such marks, including x's and parentheses, ended a sentence, I rendered them as periods. When a long dash was used to end a line, it was eliminated. If it also closed a sentence, I inserted a period. Finally, to render more readable complete thoughts or sentences not separated by punctuation or capitalization, I inserted two blank spaces between them.

ANNOTATIONS AND BIBLIOGRAPHY

A *dramatis personae* precedes the McElveen letters. Annotations of other individuals and items appear in the notes to the letters. For a complete bibliography, see all the notes. An epilogue highlights sources particularily valuable in recreating the business milieu of the Charleston slave brokers as well as the local history of Sumter District and the life of A. J. McElveen.

Notes

1. Coffin's reports originally appeared in the Boston *Daily Journal*, February through April 1865. In 1866 Coffin published his war correspondence as *Four Years of Fighting: A Volume of Personal Observation with the Army and Navy, from the First Battle of Bull Run to the Fall of Richmond* (Boston: Ticknor and Fields). In 1881 it was published under

the title *The Boys of '61, or Four Years of Fighting: A Record of Personal Observation with the Army and Navy, from the First Battle of Bull Run to the Fall of Richmond* (Boston: Estes and Lauriat). See *The National Union Catalog: Pre-1956 Imprints* (London: Mansell Information/ Publishing Limited, 1970), 114: 117. According to the catalog, the book went through ten more editions: 1882, 1883, 1884, 1885, 1886, 1888, 1891?, 1896, 1901, and 1925. The newspaper accounts do not mention any McElveen letters. For reference to "Gillmore Town," see New York *Daily Tribune*, 2 March 1865.

2. Edmund Drago and Ralph Melnick, "The Old Slave Mart Museum, Charleston, South Carolina: Rediscovering the Past," *Civil War History* 27 (June 1981): 138–54; Boston *Daily Journal*, 4 March 1865; Frederic Bancroft, *Slave-Trading in the Old South* (Baltimore: J. H. Hurst Co., 1931), 185.

3. Boston *Daily Journal*, 4 March 1865; Drago and Melnick, "The Old Slave Mart," 138–54.

4. Boston *Daily Journal*, 4 March 1865.

5. Boston *Daily Journal*, 10 March 1865.

6. New York *Daily Tribune*, 2 March 1865; Charles F. Horner, *The Life of James Redpath and the Development of the Modern Lyceum* (New York, N.Y., and Newark, N.J.: Barse and Hopkins, 1926), 7–8. I am indebted to John McKivigan for identifying Redpath's nom de plume. According to Charles Horner, Redpath was born in the "independent borough" of "Berwick-on-Tweed, on the Scottish side of the river."

7. New York *Daily Tribune*, 2 March 1865; "A Calendar and Index of Materials Presented to the Boston Public Library, 11 November 1891, by Francis Jackson Garrison," Papers of Ziba B. Oakes, Broker, of Charleston, South Carolina, 1854–1858 (Ms. Am. 322), Boston Public Library, Boston, Mass. (hereafter cited as Calendar and Index, Oakes Papers); [Francis Jackson Garrison? and Wendell Phillips Garrison?], *William Lloyd Garrison, 1805–1879: The Story of His Life Told by His Children in Four Volumes* (Boston and New York: Houghton, Mifflin and Co., 1885 and 1889), 4:134–52. There were other editions of the Garrison biography, including an 1894 one. Coffin was not alone in his desire to send mementos home. The Massachusetts Historical Society has such slave paraphernalia as a piece of an auction block, a slave collar, and whips, which formerly belonged to Governor John A. Andrew. See Andrew Collection, museum nos. 466, 446, and 452, Massachusetts Historical Society, Boston, Mass., and *Proceedings of the Massachusetts Historical Society* 54 (December 1920): 82–84.

8. Calendar and Index, Oakes Papers; Public Library of the City of Boston, Records of the Corporation, vol. 3, p. 134 (24 April 1891), Boston Public Library. See note in this book to introduction of A. J. McElveen to Z. B. Oakes, 5 June 1854, Oakes Papers.

9. Gravestones of Z. B. Oakes, Margaret Oakes, and Mary (Polly) Burrill Oakes, Magnolia Cemetery, Charleston, S.C.; Charleston County Death Records, 1821–1926 (File Card Index), Charleston County Public Library, King Street Branch, Charleston, S.C.; Charleston *Daily Courier,* 27 May 1871; Brent Holcomb, *Marriage and Death Notices from the Charleston Observer, 1827–1845* (Greenville, S.C.: A. Press, Inc., printer, 1980), 49; Charleston city directory for 1840–1841 (all Charleston city directories cited are available on microfilm at the Charleston Library Society, Charleston, S.C.); Probate Records, Suffolk County, Mass., John Christie (1816), admin., no. 24868, and Margaret G. Christie (1819), guardianship, no. 25752 (originals of all Suffolk County probate records cited are in Massachusetts Archives at Columbia Point, Boston, Mass.); Bureau of the Census, *Heads of Families at the First Census of the United States Taken in the Year 1790: Massachusetts* (Washington: Government Printing Office, 1908), 108. Until 1820 Maine was part of Massachusetts. Rachel Oakes and John Christie were married in Newcastle, Lincoln County, Maine. A Samuel Oakes appeared in the 1790 federal census for Massachusetts, but Ziba and his mother were born in Maine.

10. Charleston *Daily Courier,* 27 May 1871; Charleston city directories for 1819, 1822, 1829, 1831, 1840–1841, 1849, 1852, 1859, 1860, 1867–1868; Holcomb, *Marriage and Death Notices,* 49; South Carolina Vol. 7, p. 296, R.G. Dun & Co. Collection, Baker Library, Harvard University Graduate School of Business Administration, Soldiers Field, Boston, Mass.; Michael Tadman, *Speculators and Slaves: Masters, Traders, and Slaves in the Old South* (Madison: University of Wisconsin Press, 1989), 193 n. 21.

11. Charleston *Daily Courier,* 27 May 1871; Charleston city directories for 1855, 1867–1868, 1869–1870; gravestone of Z. B. Oakes.

12. Based on Calendar and Index, Oakes Papers, which were not completely accurate. Four letters from Greensboro, North Carolina, were mistakenly indexed as coming from South Carolina. Our statistics were corrected accordingly. Letters with no place designated were not included.

13. Manuscripts, Box 15, Diaries of Southern Trips, Frederic Bancroft Papers, Rare Book and Manuscript Library (654 Butler Library), Columbia

_____

University, New York, N.Y. Bancroft visited Charleston in 1887, 1888, 1902, 1907, 1913, and 1922.

14. Tadman, *Speculators and Slaves*, 5, 7, 30–31, 147, 170–71. Tadman's book offers the most comprehensive and up-to-date bibliography on the domestic slave trade. For an overview of the topic, see William L. Calderhead, "Slave Trade, Domestic," in Randall M. Miller and John David Smith, eds., *Dictionary of Afro-American Slavery* (Westport, Conn.: Greenwood Press, 1988), 684–89. Accounts of individual professional slave traders include: William L. Calderhead, "The Role of the Professional Slave Trader in a Slave Economy: Austin Woolfolk, Case Study," *Civil War History* 23 (September 1977): 195–211; Wendell Holmes Stephenson, *Isaac Franklin: Slave Trader and Planter of the Old South with Plantation Records* ([Baton Rouge]: Louisiana State University Press, 1938); John Allan Wyeth, *That Devil Forrest: Life of General Bedford Forrest* (New York: Harper and Brothers, 1959; Baton Rouge: Louisiana State University Press, Louisiana Paperback Edition, 1989). The Wyeth book was first published in 1899.

15. Tadman, *Speculators and Slaves*, 31, 33, 132, 168, 192–204.

16. Tadman, *Speculators and Slaves*, 132, 168; Leighton and Sherman to Z. B. Oakes, 20 December 1856, and E. A. Edwards to Z. B. Oakes, 14 April 1857, with enclosure, Oakes Papers.

17. Bancroft, *Slave-Trading in the Old South*, 167–69, 186; Oakes family plot; Holcomb, *Marriage and Death Notices*, 49; Population Schedules of the Seventh Census of the United States, 1850, South Carolina, Charleston District, pp. 116, 220, Records of the Bureau of the Census, National Archives, Washington, D.C., (hereafter the federal censuses shall be cited as follows: U.S. Census, year, state, district/county, page nos.); U.S. Census, 1860, S.C., Charleston, 293A; Probate Records, Suffolk County, Mass., John Christie (1816), admin., no. 24868, and Francis Garaux (1840), admin., no. 32390; American Antiquarian Society, comp., *Index of Marriages in Massachusetts Centinel and Columbian Centinel, 1784–1840* (Boston: G. K. Hall Co., 1961), 2: 1332, 1424; Charleston city directories for 1835–1836, 1849, 1852, 1855, 1859, 1867–1868, 1869–1870, 1886; Estate Files, Ziba B. Oakes (1892), admin., no. 360–3, and Marriage Licenses, John S. Riggs and Mattie Reynolds Marshall (1878), no. 100312, both in Charleston County Probate Court, Charleston, S.C. For the wealth of the two men, see *List of the Tax Payers of the City of Charleston for 1859* (Charleston: Walker, Evans and Co., 1860), and *List of the Tax Payers of the City of Charleston*

for 1860 (Charleston: Evans and Cogswell, 1861). In 1860 Oakes owned sixteen slaves and real estate worth $72,500. His sister Charlotte had married a merchant and in 1850 ran a boarding house. Margaret Oakes was probably named after the wife of Francis Garaux, a Boston baker who was appointed an appraiser of her father's estate at his death. Margaret and Ziba's daughter Josephine married a carpet dealer, Samer S. Howell, whose father was in the dry goods, then insurance, business. After the war, Samer was a commission merchant, and later a traveling salesman.

18. A. J. McElveen to Z. B. Oakes, 4 August, 9 December 1853, 30 August 1856, Oakes Papers; Charleston *Mercury*, 17 January 1853.

19. Bruce F. Morrison, "The Influence of the Railroad on the Rural Settlement Landscape of Sumter County, South Carolina: 1848–1978" (M.A. thesis, Department of Geography, University of South Carolina, 1980); Frederick Burtrum Collins, Jr., "Charleston and the Railroads: A Geographic Study of a South Atlantic Port and Its Strategies for Developing a Railroad System, 1820–1860" (M.S. thesis, Department of Geography, University of South Carolina, 1977); A. J. McElveen to Z. B. Oakes, 18 August 1853, 24 April 1854, 19 November 1854, Oakes Papers; Sumter (Sumterville) *Black River Watchman*, 11 November 1853.

20. Lacy K. Ford, Jr., *Origins of Southern Radicalism: The South Carolina Upcountry, 1800–1860* (New York: Oxford University Press, 1988), 235–37, 315–20.

21. Sumter *Watchman*, 23 July 1856; T. L. Gelser to Z. B. Oakes, 12 April 1854, J. B. Witherspoon to Z. B. Oakes, 10 September 1854, Oakes Papers. See Robley Dunglison, A *Dictionary of Medical Science*, enlarged and revised by Richard J. Dunglison (Philadelphia: Henry C. Lea, 1874), 180, 333, for a nineteenth-century medical definition of dysmenorrhea, or dysmenorrhoea. According to Dunglison, dysmenorrhoea was painful menstruation "very difficult of removal." The condition prevented conception and required "the liberal use of narcotics."

22. Tadman, *Speculators and Slaves*, 193 n. 21; Charleston city directories for 1867–1868, 1869–1870; Charleston *Daily News and Courier*, 4 February 1899. For the extent of the fortunes of the Riggs and Oakes families, see Estate Files, Z. B. Oakes (1871), will, no. 205-15, and John S. Riggs (1899), will, no. 423-24, Charleston County Probate Court, and South Carolina Vol. 7, p. 296, R.G. Dun & Co. Collection. In the 1869–1870 city directory, Riggs was listed as a commission agent, auctioneer, real estate broker, and "stock and exchange" broker, as well as president of the City Railway Company.

---

23. F. L. Cardozo to Messrs. Whipple and Strieby, 3 October 1866, American Missionary Association Archives, 1821–1891, Amistad Research Center, Tulane University, New Orleans, La.; South Carolina Vol. 6, p. 212, R.G. Dun & Co. Collection; S. S. Riggs to F. Bancroft, 31 July 1922, 24 July 1924, Correspondence with S. S. Riggs, M. F. Kennedy, in Domestic Slave Trade Documents, Manuscripts, Box 12, Negro and Slavery—Notes, etc., Frederic Bancroft Papers. Sidney Riggs was in the real estate business. The two "modern" hotels just completed to accommodate tourists and business people were the Francis Marion and Fort Sumter. The latter, "built on Charleston's sacred ground 'The Battery,'" had a splendid view of the ocean and surrounding rivers. In the entrepreneurial tradition of his father, Sidney Riggs, recalling Frederic Bancroft's inquiries two years earlier, perceived the money-making potential of the slave mart as a tourist attraction. Renewing his correspondence with the historian, he asked if the book on Charleston was completed.

24. Coffin, *Four Years of Fighting*, 474–75. Tadman, *Speculators and Slaves*, 38 n. 27, noted only 103 McElveen to Oakes letters. Of the six additional letters, one was from McElveen to another person; three were addressed to McElveen; and two came from other people with the surname McElveen.

25. Michael P. Johnson and James L. Roark, *Black Masters: A Free Family of Color in the Old South* (New York: W. W. Norton and Co., 1984), 339; Anne King Gregorie, *History of Sumter County, South Carolina* (Sumter, S.C.: Library Board of Sumter County, 1954), 3–4, 171, 231–32; Morrison, "The Influence of the Railroad," 16–17, 20–23. Sandy Grove became part of Clarendon District. According to Morrison, 665 square miles presently compose Sumter County.

26. The Compromise of 1808 "established a *de facto* balance of power between the Upcountry and the Lowcountry." See Ford, *Origins of Southern Radicalism*, 106–107, especially note 20; and Gregorie, *History of Sumter County*, 3.

27. Nexsen Johnson, "Some Williamsburg County Names," *Names in South Carolina* 16 (Winter 1969): 39; William Willis Boddie, *History of Williamsburg: Something about the People of Williamsburg County, South Carolina, from the First Settlement by Europeans about 1705 until 1923* (Columbia, S.C.: State Co., 1923), 38–40; Janie Revill, *Sumter District* ([Columbia, S.C.?]: State Printing Co., printer, 1968), 2, 23; Dalton K. Brasington, Jr., "A Historical Geography of South Carolina's Inner Coastal Plain Cotton Region" (M.A. thesis, Department of Geog-

raphy, University of South Carolina, 1977), 23. For a discussion of British folkways including Scotch-Irish, see David Hackett Fischer, *Albion Seed: Four British Folkways in America* (New York: Oxford University Press, 1989). Mr. W. Esmonde Howell of Sumter County recalled Margaret McElveen's remark. Miss McElveen did genealogical research on both the Frierson and McElveen families. John Frierson IV of Pudding Swamp married Jane McElveen. See Margaret R. McElveen, "The Ancestry and Children of John Frierson of Shiloh, S.C.," typed paper, in Sumter County Public Library, Sumter, S.C.; "Bible Records of the R. L. McElveen Family," Sumter County Genealogical Society, Sumter, S.C.; and I. E. Lowery, *Life on the Old Plantation in Antebellum Days or a Story Based on Facts* (Columbia, S.C.: State Co., 1911), 29, 37. Rachel N. Klein, *Unification of a Slave State: The Rise of the Planter Class in the South Carolina Backcountry, 1760–1808* (Chapel Hill: University of North Carolina Press, 1990) described the transformation of the backcountry before the spread of the cotton economy. She noted the tensions between early settlers who relied primarily on hunting for their subsistence and those who did not. See chapter 1.

28. Revill, *Sumter District*, 23; Ralph H. Ramsey, Jr., and A. H. Green, *Sumter County: Economic and Social* (Columbia: University of South Carolina, 1922), 15–16; *The Outlook*, 23 May 1914, pp. 196–97, as quoted in Manuscripts, Box 11, Negro and Slavery — Notes, etc., pp. A177–A178, Frederic Bancroft Papers. On 31 January 1853, the Charleston *Mercury* published a report by the directors of the South Carolina Railroad Company that for the past six months the company had suffered heavy losses because of the fever in Charleston and "great Freshets" in August. The damage caused by these freshets, which temporarily "cut off all communication entirely between Charleston and the interior," was repaired "almost exclusively by our own hands and the Road force, (for we could get no others that would undergo the risk and exposure of working at that season in the water and swamps)."

29. "Bible Records of the R. L. McElveen Family"; Gregorie, *History of Sumter County*, 12; Revolutionary War Pension and Bounty Land Warrant Application Files, William McElveen, service S.C., no. S21880, National Archives; South Carolina Land Grants, William McElveen, Sr. (1804), vol. 50, pp. 384–85, South Carolina Department of Archives and History, Columbia, S.C.; Plat Files, William McElveen, Sr. (1804), vol. MP, pp. 587, 691, Sumter County Register of Mesne Conveyance, Sumter, S.C.; Boddie, *History of Williamsburg*, 185–86; Estate Files,

William McElveen, Sr. (1837), admin., bundle 64, package 3, Sumter County Probate Court (Office of Probate Judge), Sumter, S.C. The petition of administration of McElveen's estate was read publicly at Midway Church.

30. Revolutionary War Pension and Bounty Land Warrant Application Files, William McElveen, service S.C., no. S21880; Estate Files, William McElveen, Sr. (1837), admin., bundle 64, package 3, Sumter County Probate Court; Conveyance Files, Heirs of William McElveen, Sr. (1838), vol. II, pp. 650–52, Sumter County Register of Mesne Conveyance. The appraised value of McElveen's estate at his death was about twenty-three hundred dollars. However, the market value was considerably less. The two slaves appraised at $750.00 were sold for $500.50.

31. Janie Revill, *President Andrew Jackson's Birthplace As Found by Janie Revill* (Columbia, S.C.: State Printing Co., 1966). A. J. McElveen to Z. B. Oakes, 3 October, 27 October 1853, 29 November, 1 December, 4 December 1854, 8 July, 10 July, 13 August, 30 August 1856, 29 March 1857, Oakes Papers; Conveyance Files, A. J. McElveen, (1852) vol. O, pp. 355–56, 359–60, (1855) vol. P, pp. 390–91, (1857) vol. Q, pp. 8–9, and Joseph Chandler, (1857) vol. Q, pp. 9–11, Sumter County Register of Mesne Conveyance; South Carolina Vol. 13, p. 68K, R.G. Dun & Co. Collection. There is an A. J. McElveen in the 1870 manuscript census returns for Privateer Township, Sumter County. See U.S. Census, 1870, S.C., Sumter, 138. I am assuming that the 135 letters in the Oakes collection were written by Andrew J. McElveen. On 4 March 1857, A. J. wrote he was sending Oakes seven slaves. He said that he was bound only for Carter, Harriet, Powell, and Emily; all four slaves were mentioned specifically by name in a $5,000 mortgage (Andrew J. McElveen to W. F. B. Haynseworth, Comr. Eq.) recorded in the same month and year. The other three slaves, Smart, Mary, and Simon, belonging to Joseph Chandler, were mentioned in another mortgage (Joseph Chandler to W. F. B. Haynseworth, Comr. Eq.) also recorded on the same date. I cannot determine exactly how Andrew J. McElveen was related to William McElveen, Sr. Local historian Margaret R. McElveen did not mention A. J. (Andrew J.) McElveen in her extensively researched genealogy of the McElveen clan. My query about A. J. (Andrew J.) McElveen in the newsletter of the Sumter County Genealogical Society, *Sumter Black River Watchman*, 15 (April 1990): 3, went unanswered.

For the McElveen-Mellett connection, see Conveyance Files, Frances H. Mellett and Andrew J. McElveen to William Lewis, deed of settlement, recorded 9 October 1855, vol. PP, pp. 69-72, Sumter County

Register of Mesne Conveyance; Estate Files, James L. Mellett (1853), will, bundle 134, package 3, Sumter County Probate Court; Cassie Nicholes, *Historical Sketches of Sumter County: Its Birth and Growth* (Sumter, S.C.: Sumter County Historical Commission, 1975), 1: 344–46. The family name Mellett was also spelled Mellette.

32. Stephenson, *Isaac Franklin*; Wyeth, *That Devil Forrest*, chapter 1; Tadman, *Speculators and Slaves*, 193, 259. Charleston broker A. J. Salinas began his career as a clerk for another Charleston broker, T. N. Gadsden.

33. A. J. McElveen to Z. B. Oakes, 27 October 1853, 16 May, 6 July, 1 September 1854, Oakes Papers.

34. For details on "Old Fogyism," see Ford, *Origins of Southern Radicalism*, 315–24. Efforts to repeal the state's usury laws ultimately failed. For references on the railroad operations on Sunday, see Charleston *Mercury*, 9 February, 10 February 1853; *Jas. E. Calhoun on the Sabbath Question*, ca. 1853, pamphlet no. 385, South Carolina Historical Society, Charleston, S.C. (the title page was missing); Sumter (Sumterville) *Black River Watchman*, 10 March 1854. The "speedy repair" involved 200 hands working in the swamp on Sunday.

35. A. J. McElveen to Z. B. Oakes, 27 October 1853, 30 August 1854, Oakes Papers.

36. A. J. McElveen to Z. B. Oakes, 4 August, 3 October 1853, 1 December, 4 December 1854, 3 February 1855, 2 August, 21 October 1856, Oakes Papers. The railroads mentioned in the letters are the Wilmington and Manchester, and the South Carolina, including the Columbia Road (Branch).

37. J. A. Weatherly to Z. B. Oakes, 7 August 1856, A. J. McElveen to Z. B. Oakes, 6 January 1852, 13 July, 9 August 1853, 19 January, 31 January, 7 February, 6 June 1854, Oakes Papers.

38. A. J. McElveen to Z. B. Oakes, 22 October 1853, 23 August 1854, 13 August, 1 September, 16 September, 15 October (Bamberg), 15 October (Montgomery), 4 November, 2 December 1856, Oakes Papers.

39. A. J. McElveen to Z. B. Oakes, 14 October, 22 October, 27 October 1853, 15 May, 6 June, 6 July 1854, Oakes Papers. McElveen's sentiments affirm Bertram Wyatt-Brown's analysis in his book, *Southern Honor: Ethics and Behavior in the Old South* (New York: Oxford University Press, 1982; Oxford University Press paperback, 1983).

40. A. J. McElveen to Z. B. Oakes, 20 November 1856, 7 January, 21 February, 7 March, 22 March 1857, Oakes Papers.

41. South Carolina Vol. 13, p. 68K, R.G. Dun & Co. Collection; Compiled Service Records of Confederate Soldiers Who Served in Organizations

from the State of South Carolina, Fourth State Troops (Six Months, 1863–1864), I–S, A. J. McElveen, and Fifth Reserves (Ninety Days, 1862–1863), T–Y through Fifth Militia, A. J. McElveen, National Archives; Nicholes, *Historical Sketches*, 1: 346.

42. South Carolina Vol. 13, p. 68K, R.G. Dun & Co. Collection; Conveyance Files, A. J. McElveen, (1869) vol. S, p. 360, (1870) vol. SS, pp. 586–87, Sumter County Register of Mesne Conveyance; Gregorie, *History of Sumter County*, 285–86, 475; U.S. Census, 1870, S.C., Sumter, 138.

43. Nicholes, *Historical Sketches*, 1: 346; U.S. Census, 1870, S.C., Sumter, 138; Conveyance Files, J. D. McElveen from Paul S. Felder (1885), vol. Z, p. 233, and John S. Richardson, Master-in-Equity, to Daniel A. Outlaw (1892), title, vol. FFF, pp. 254–55, Sumter County Register of Mesne Conveyance. According to Nicholes, Dr. James L. Mellett was buried near Privateer (probably the town). In 1885 a J. D. McElveen purchased a parcel of land in Privateer Township "bounded North by lands of Andrew J. McElveen East by lands of Francis Compton." A farm laborer named John Compton was living in the household of A. J. McElveen in 1870. In the dispute over the 169⅓ acres of land in Privateer Township, the plaintiff was Jefferson Davis McElveen and the defendants were "William F. O. McElvene and Others." Because of this dispute the land was sold for twelve hundred dollars to D. A. Outlaw in 1892. See Index to Conveyances, Real Estate, Sumter County, S.C., from 29 April 1887 to 1 January 1904, p. 456, Sumter County Register of Mesne Conveyance. It describes the parties involved in this 1892 transaction as "McElveen, A. J. Children to D. A. Outlaw."

44. Ira Berlin, ed., et al., *Freedom: A Documentary History of Emancipation, 1861-1867, Selected from the Holdings of the National Archives of the United States. Series II, The Black Military Experience* (Cambridge: Cambridge University Press, 1982). The project was "a systematic search of those records at the National Archives that promised to yield material for a documentary history of emancipation."

Dramatis Personae

Belser. Lawrence H. Belser, planter and slave trader, Manchester, Sumter District.[1]

Benbow. H. L. Benbow and W. W. Benbow, farmers, Clarendon, Sumter District. H. L. lived at Wright's Bluff.[2]

Briscoe. E. C. Briscoe, slave trader, Port Gibson, Mississippi.[3]

Brown. S. N. Brown, slave trader, Montgomery, Alabama.[4]

Burgess. William Sidney Burgess, physician, Middle Salem, Sumter District. Samuel A. Burgess, planter, Pudding Swamp, Sumter District (later Clarendon). Samuel helped found Manning, the "new courthouse village" of Clarendon District.[5]

Burch Kirkland and Co. Montgomery firm with which McElveen did business when he traveled west.[6]

Burkett. Henry G. Burkett, overseer and slave trader, Middle Salem, Sumter District. He was held in low esteem by A. J. McElveen.[7]

Caleb. Slave purchased by McElveen for Oakes from H. Bethune of Clarendon, Sumter District. In March 1854 Caleb was sold to William T. Whaley, Jr., of John's Island, across the Ashley River from Charleston. By early June Caleb had run away; six months later he was apprehended and jailed in Kingstree.[8]

Chandler Family. Joseph and James R. Chandler (planters), and Robert A. Chandler (school teacher), Stony Run, Sumter District. A transaction involving the Chandlers might have led to a lawsuit for McElveen.[9]

Doss. Slave blacksmith whom McElveen failed to sell or ex-

change over a period of seventeen months (1853–1855). Mc-
Elveen took Doss to Darlington and left him with the farmer
George J. W. McCall, who could not sell him. Eventually,
G. W. White, a farmer from Williamsburg District, took
Doss west (Alabama) to sell for McElveen. Unsuccessful, he
left Doss in Hamburg, Alabama, with the trader John K.
White, who also could not find an immediate buyer.[10]

Gilchrist. Probably John M. Gilchrist, Charleston broker and
auctioneer, 11 State Street.[11]

Green Family. Major William M. Green, farmer, and Henry D.
Green, physician, brothers from Bishopville, Sumter District.[12]

Henry. Prime field hand who immediately ran away after being bought by McElveen for $925 in February 1854. Ap-
prehended in March, he was not sold until July 1854 for
nearly the same price.[13]

Ingram. John I. Ingram, a Sumter District physician, consulted
by McElveen to certify the soundness of slaves. Ingram, a
state senator "highly respected," played an important role
in the establishment of Clarendon District in 1855.[14]

James. Slave taken by McElveen in 1856 to be sold in Alabama, where he feigned being "unsound." McElveen arranged
for Burch Kirkland and Company of Montgomery to em-
ploy him temporarily at a local livery stable. When the
stable owner threatened to "correct" James for misbehavior
without the company's approval, the slave ran away on a
stolen horse. He was apprehended and returned to Burch
Kirkland and Company, which sent him back to Oakes.[15]

Joe. Slave bought by McElveen in 1853 and involved in a dispute over his alleged unsoundness (see McRae below). In
1856 he ran away for several months but McElveen employed trackers and bloodhounds to find him.[16]

"Little Oakes." Son of A. J. McElveen.

McCauley. Probably James McCauley, physician, Clarendon,
Sumter District.[17]

McElveen. H. Elijah McElveen, Shiloh, and W. H. McElveen, Sandy Grove, both in Sumter District in 1850. A planter, Elijah McElveen, lived in Pudding Swamp, Sumter District (later Clarendon). He was probably a slave trader. In 1850 an overseer, William H. McElveen, resided in the household of his father William McElveen, a wealthy planter. W. H. also operated a Sumter grocery store and was in the slave trade with H. G. Burkett.[18]

McLeod Family. The McLeod brothers, Napoleon and Robert L., Clarendon, Sumter District. Robert resided near the present-day city of Manning. In 1850 he was a planter while Napoleon was an overseer. By 1860 both were listed as farmers.[19]

McRae. G. W. A. McRae, physician, Effingham, Darlington District. He sold Joe to McElveen. Joe was then sold to A. N. McKay, who probably was from Graham's Turnout in Barnwell District. When McKay discovered that Joe had a venereal disease, McRae refused to take him back. The doctor claimed that Joe had been sound when he sold him. Furthermore, Joe might have been "injured by improper treatment perhaps . . . with Mercury" for the disease. McElveen suggested the issue be tested in the court in Sumterville. In 1856 Joe was working for McElveen.[20]

Manser. H. Manser, slave trader, Richmond, Virginia.[21]

Moses. Probably Colonel Montgomery Moses, a lawyer and the Sumterville agent for the Bank of the State of South Carolina. He practiced law with his brother Israel Franklin Moses (known as "F. J. Moses"). Sumterville merchant A. J. (Andrew Jackson) Moses was also interested in banking.[22]

Richardson. John S. Richardson, Jr., lawyer, Middle Salem, Sumter District. He was also an editor and owner of the Sumter *Banner*.[23]

Riggs. John S. Riggs, Jr., Charleston broker and auctioneer, 4 State Street.[24]

Ryan. John S. Ryan, Charleston broker and auctioneer, 22 Broad Street. W. K. Ryan, Charleston factor and commission merchant, Boyce and Company's Wharf.[25]

Sharp. John M. E. Sharpe, slave trader and merchant, Columbia, Richland District.[26]

Susan. Close acquaintance of Oakes family courted by A. J. McElveen.

Weatherly. Probably Thomas C. Weatherly, slave trader and farmer, Bennettsville, Marlboro District.[27]

Whiteside. James H. Whiteside, slave trader, Coates Tavern, York District. He sometimes worked for Oakes.[28]

Witherspoon. J. B. Witherspoon, a wealthy and respected Sumterville doctor.[29]

Notes

1. L. H. Belser to Z. B. Oakes, 15 April, 20 May 1857, Oakes Papers; Tadman, *Speculators and Slaves,* 39–40, 277.
2. Dorothy O. Teel, comp., *1860 Census, Clarendon District, South Carolina* (Hemingway, S.C.: Three Rivers Historical Society, 1983), dws. [dwellings] 265, 267; H. L. Benbow to Z. B. Oakes, 4 March 1855, Oakes Papers.
3. E. C. Briscoe to Z. B. Oakes, 26 March 1854, 30 March [1854?], 8 March 1857, Oakes Papers.
4. S. N. Brown to Z. B. Oakes, 25 December [1854?], 5 January, 2 March 1855, Oakes Papers; Tadman, *Speculators and Slaves,* 40, 265; Bancroft, *Slave-Trading in the Old South,* 297, 381. According to Tadman, Brown was from Kershaw District.
5. Dorothy O. Teel, [comp.], *1850 Census, Sumter-District, South Carolina* (Hemingway, S.C.: Three Rivers Historical Society, 1983), dws. 1460, 1638; Teel, *1860 Census, Clarendon District,* dw. 624; Gregorie, *History of Sumter County,* 231.
6. A. J. McElveen to Z. B. Oakes, 1 November 1856, Burch Kirkland and Company to Z. B. Oakes, 15, 20, 22, 29 November 1856, Oakes Papers.
7. A. J. McEleveen to Z. B. Oakes, 29 July, 22 October, 13 December 1853, 1 May, 3 May 1854, Oakes Papers; Teel, *1850 Census, Sumter-District,* dw. 1203.

---

8. A. J. McElveen to Z. B. Oakes, 7 June, 1 December 1854, 24 February, 26 February, 8 March 1855, W. T. Whaley, Jr., to Z. B. Oakes, 5 June 1854, 2 March 1855, W. R. Wilson to Z. B. Oakes, 22 February 1855, Oakes Papers.

9. Teel, *1850 Census, Sumter-District*, dws. 1790–92; A. J. McElveen to Z. B. Oakes, 2, 4, 7, 16, 22, 28 March, 4, 18, 22 April 1857, Oakes Papers; Conveyance Files, vol. Q, pp. 8–11, Sumter County Register of Mesne Conveyance.

10. A. J. McElveen to Z. B. Oakes, 9 August, 20 August, 10, 12, 27 October 1853, 17 July, 9 September, 11, 18, 19, 24, 29 November, 11 December 1854, 6 January, 13 January 1855, J. K. White to Z. B. Oakes and A. J. McElveen, 23 January 1855, Oakes Papers; U.S. Census, 1850, S.C., Darlington, 349, and Williamsburg, 118.

11. J. King to Z. B. Oakes, 19 February, 30 May 1854, Oakes Papers; Tadman, *Speculators and Slaves*, 40, 255; Charleston city directory (1855), 41.

12. W. M. Green to Z. B. Oakes, 19 February, 28 February 1855, A. J. McElveen to Z. B. Oakes, 23 December 1854, 7, 24, 26, 28 February 1855, Oakes Papers; Teel, *1860 Census, Sumter-District*, dws. 4, 187.

13. A. J. McElveen to Z. B. Oakes, 7 February, 11 February, 6, [8?], 13, 15, 22 March, 14, 21, 24 April, 1, 3, 10, 27 May, 6 June, 17 July 1854, Oakes Papers.

14. Certificate by John I. Ingram, 8 November 1853, A. J. McElveen to Z. B. Oakes, 7 November, 8 November, 9 December 1853, Oakes Papers; Nicholes, *Historical Sketches*, 1: 111–12.

15. A. J. McElveen to Z. B. Oakes, 21 October, 1 November, 2 December 1856, 9 January 1857, Burch Kirkland and Company to Z. B. Oakes, 15, 20, 22 November 1856, Oakes Papers.

16. A. J. McElveen to Z. B. Oakes, 10 October 1853, 13 August, 30 August, 8 September 1856, Oakes Papers.

17. Gregorie, *History of Sumter County*, 161–62; Teel, *1850 Census, Sumter-District*, dw. 352.

18. Tadman, *Speculators and Slaves*, 271, 273, 279; Teel, *1850 Census, Sumter-District*, dws. 1635, 1692; Teel, *1860 Census, Sumter-District*, dw. 719 (717); Teel, *1860 Census, Clarendon District*, dw. 828; South Carolina Vol. 13, p. 63, R.G. Dun & Co. Collection. A. J. McElveen mentions McElveens without giving their first names. His references to them do not even suggest that they were directly related to him.

19. Teel, *1850 Census, Sumter-District*, dws. 923, 1446; Teel, *1860 Census, Clarendon District*, dws. 764, 878; Certificate by John I. Ingram,

8 November 1853, A. J. McElveen to Z. B. Oakes, 9 December 1853, Oakes Papers; South Carolina Vol. 13, p. 68A, R.G. Dun & Co. Collection.

20. A. N. McKay to Z. B. Oakes, 26 September 1854, G. W. A. McRae to Z. B. Oakes, 11 August 1854, A. J. McElveen to Z. B. Oakes, 10 October 1853, 13, 15, 16, 18, 27, 29 May, 25 July, 10 August, 23 August 1854, 13 August, 30 August, 8 September 1856, Oakes Papers; Claude Henry Neuffer, ed., *Names in South Carolina: Volumes I–XII, 1954–1965* (Columbia: Department of English, University of South Carolina, 1967), 79. When the Seaboard Railroad between Columbia and Savannah was built in 1891, Graham's Turnout, located on this line, was renamed Denmark in honor of a railroad promoting family.

21. Tadman, *Speculators and Slaves*, 273.

22. Gregorie, *History of Sumter County*, 94–95, 103–104, 126, 241, 540; Sumter (Sumterville) *Banner*, 6 January [1847] (mistakenly typed as 1846), 7 August 1850, 21 September 1852; Teel, *1850 Census, Sumter-District*, dws. 1851, 1857, 1858.

23. A. J. McElveen to Z. B. Oakes, 29 July 1853, 27 May, 30 May 1854, J. S. Richardson, Jr., to Z. B. Oakes, 28 July, 17 August 1853, Oakes Papers; Sumter (Sumterville) *Banner*, 5 July 1854, 7 February 1855; Gregorie, *History of Sumter County*, 246, 454–55, 545.

24. Charleston city directory (1855), 89.

25. Charleston city directory (1855), 92–93.

26. Tadman, *Speculators and Slaves*, 40, 270, 281.

27. Tadman, *Speculators and Slaves*, 40, 94, 267, 282; Calendar and Index, Oakes Papers.

28. A. J. McElveen to Z. B. Oakes, 29 December 1854, J. H. Whiteside to Z. B. Oakes, 21 July 1854, Oakes Papers; U.S. Census, 1860, S.C., York, 384.

29. J. B. Witherspoon to Z. B. Oakes, 10 September 1854, A. J. McElveen to Z. B. Oakes, 11 September 1854, Oakes Papers; Sumter *Watchman*, 23 July 1856; Michael P. Johnson and James L. Roark, eds., *No Chariot Let Down: Charleston's Free People of Color on the Eve of the Civil War* (Chapel Hill: University of North Carolina Press, 1984; New York: W. W. Norton and Co. paperback, 1986), 142 n. 29; Teel, *1850 Census, Sumter-District*, dw. 1877; Teel, *1860 Census, Sumter-District*, dw. 380.

McELVEEN LETTERS,
1852–1857

*"You were never anything but a
hard-working drummer who landed in the ash can
like all the rest of them!"*
Biff to Willy Loman,
Death of a Salesman by Arthur Miller.

"Broke by the war — old man."
R.G. Dun & Co. on A. J. McElveen, 1871.

A. J. McElveen to Z. B. Oakes,
Sumterville, S.C., 6 January 1852. (262)

it is with pleasure I drop you a line hoping they will find you and famly in fine health   they leave me in Tolerable health   I have Bin very unwell Since I left the City but almost Retains my former vigor.   I am Going a head in Business   I Bought only Ten head yesterday and Give Thundering prices for them   I think I can Save myself By your assistance   I Trust you will be a friend to me one more   I have laid out but little money in the Purchase   I intend to try and lay out all the money you Sent me to day   on my way down I will take the negroes down By my own Conveyance to Save Expences   I want to be in town on Saturday or Sunday provide the weather will admit   I have 3 fellows a woman and five children   a boy large Enough to Plow a Girl large Enough to nurse and three smaller one to the Brest   the mother ordernary   I have one Single Girl. please Excuse me for not Sending anny down   before this I could not See any Bargains   I will State all particulars when I come.

A. J. McElveen to Z. B. Oakes,
Sumterville, S.C., 10 July 1853. (216)

I Send you one Boy which I hope will please you well.   I think he is as near no 1 as Boys Get   The price I think is rather high.   I hope he will pay a tolerable profit   it is the best that can be done   Boy wilson Bought of Mr Semore I paid Seven hundred & Seventy five Dollars.   I hope you will be able to Get $900 for him.   I refused a Girl 20 years of age at $700 yesterday   I offred $675 for her   I think it Enough.   if you think Best to take her at $700 I can Still Get her   She is very Badley whipt but good teeth   the

---

whipping has bin done long Since   She is tolerably likely.
the Prices up here is tall   they ask from $950 to $1000 for
fellows and Eight for girls Generally.   this Boy wilson I
weighd him   his weigt is 100 lbs By the Scales this Evening.
I will try and have Some more next week   do let me here
from you   I leave here thursday for below   I will return
next week

A. J. McElveen to Z. B. Oakes,
Sumterville, S.C., 13 July 1853. (215)

I haste to drop you a line hoping it will meet you and
famly all well   I Sent down a boy this morning which I
hope will Reach you Safe   I could not write to let you Know
before Sending   I hope you will Excuse me   I did not
wish to detain the Boy as you directed me to Send as fast as
I Bought   do try and Send to the cars Every day as it is not
in my power to write Every time To inform you.   I wrote
By the Boy which I hope you will Recd on his landing Safe.
Should he not arrive Safe you can Identify him By one of his
Big toes being off.   I hope that will not be any objections
to his Selling   I could not Get one dollar nocked off for
that   I dont think it Should lessen his value   he is no 1
Boy in appearance, and I cant By such for less Price here.
I think he ought to Sell as well as a fellow   he weighs 100
lbs.   {Sell him for $900 if Posible}   I will try and leave
mon next week   write me next week and Give me all the
Points necessary
P.S I paid $775 for Wilson.

A. J. McElveen to Z. B. Oakes,
Sumterville, S.C., 29 July 1853. (206)

your letters was duly Received and contents noticed   in
the first place I am very Sorry I Sent you Such pore Stock,

but I am in hopes you will be able to Get a little advance on them.   I Send you a Girl named betsy[1] which I hope will Give Every Satisfaction   Bought of Mr M mims of Darlington Dist   I paid $785 the least dollar could Bye her. I hope I will Get her Brother at 700   weighs 100 lbs   his master ask me $750   he is likely Except Bad teeth   perhaps I may not Get him until monday.   I will do my best to Get the fellows for you, but it is hard matter to Bye at any price.   Burkett met with a trader from Louisana Since he left town and what I could learn is trying to Get him a lot of negros   Sharp Sent him over to See burkett   I want as little to do with burkett as posible   Mr Dixion happened to Meet me here to day and Says he cant Sell yet   he promised me to try and Get me one fellow next week   do Say what is the hiest price you can Give for Mr Richardson boy[2] as he is anxious to Sell him.   as for the man Returning Charlott & Roxanne[3] let him do So and then he will See where he will Get his Redress   I dont ask him any favours   if he writes to me I will Give him a [cutter?] and learn him a lesson.   if you Should See him tell him I am Ready to Meet him at any time or place, and if he wants any Redress tell him to come to me   dont take the negros Back attall   I believe Every thing was fairly under Stood as to the Situation of the negros   write me on Recept of this

P.S. Mr Oakes if you will let me take the chances I can

---

1. Betsy was subsequently sent to a trading firm in Mississippi. See A. J. McElveen to Z. B. Oakes, 10 October 1853, Oakes Papers, and note 16 below.
2. John S. Richardson, Jr., was the trustee of an estate for which he was charged to sell a slave named Phillip. J. S. Richardson, Jr., to Z. B. Oakes, 28 July, 17 August 1853, Oakes Papers.
3. Charlott and Roxanne were sold by Oakes to W. Nicholson, Chester Court House, Chester District. Nicholson complained that Charlott had medical problems. W. Nicholson to Z. B. Oakes, 27 July 1853, Oakes Papers.

Sell or Exchange the Girl Emley[4]   do Send her up on monday   I will See Good many persons out and Il try and En-
gage her that day   I donot wish any money lost on my pur-
chese   not thinking to mention this I Broke the letter open
after it was Sealed

A. J. McElveen to Z. B. Oakes,
Sumterville, S.C., 4 August 1853. (201)

yours came Safe to hand   I am Glad to here you have
men wating for Stock   I have 4 Boys   I hope to Get them
down Safe as I wrote you the other day   I here this Evening
the R.R. is Broken down and I am fearful It will be trobled
to Get them down Safe   I will put this in the mail as I Suppose it will be Sent any how and if I can Get the negros on
I will See them to the Columbia Road and if they dont Get
down you will Know the Reason.   primus tolerable likely
fellow   a little whipt I am fearful will be objected to   he
taulks well   he weighs 165 lbs   Sam weighs 132 lbs
James weighs 88 lbs   prince weighs 53   prices primus
$900, Sam & James, Bought together $1500   prince 470
Mr Oakes I hope they will Suit the market tolerable well and
I trust you will make a good profit on them.   I wish you
to Send me fifteen hundred Dollars or make arrangements
with the Bank So I can Get what I need   I cant draw the
hole amount at once   I owe fifteen hundred for this lot and
I have Bought too more fellows at $1000 Each which I will Get
on Saturday if the Boys dont Runaway   Col Moses Seams
to Grumble with out   he was fully Satisfied how the letter
of credid Runs   his Brother are Gone to the north and he

---

4. Emley was placed with a family on trial in August and was sold in November 1853 to the McFaddins of Sumter District. See A. J. McElveen
to Z. B. Oakes, 29 August, 9 November 1853, 17 July 1854, Oakes Papers.

Says he never Seen my letter of credit   please Send me the
money immediatly   they too fellow I Bought will Get them
on Saturday   I would had them know if I could Got them
without the money but I had to come here and draw it before
I could Bye them   the too fellows will fill the order I Reced
from you   no 1 Boys.

A. J. McElveen to Z. B. Oakes,
Sumterville, S.C., 7 August 1853. (199)

　　your draft and letters was duly Recd this Evening   I
am Glad to here the negros arrived Safe but I am Sorry to See
they did not Pay a better profit   I Thought Sure primus Sam
& James was Good for three hundred Dollars profit   Such
Boys ought to Bring the hiest market Price   it is very Seldom I can Get Such Stock.   do the Best you can   I cant
complaine   I am Sorry I failed in Geting the 2 fellows
one the title is not Good   the other his master Backed out
as usual By not having the money to Plank down.   they are
one Runaway which I am Sure of Getting   his master put
out word if he would come to me he would let him off   I
Give him until Tuesday to come to me   if he dont come I
will have the Blood hound after him as Soon as I can Get there
from Darlington   the Boy is willing to Go with me   he
is no 1   20 years   weight a bout 175   near Six feet.
look for more Stock for I am Sure to have Some Soon
　　I have Emly yet   I hope to Sell her to morrow   if
not I have a chance to Exchange her for a Boy as Soon as I
have time to See the Gentleman   I have Bin So Busy I could
not Get to See him.   The weather is So disagreeable I can
hardly Get a bout and my horse are near done down   we
have Rain Every day and it is Schorching hot.   Give my
Respects to the famly   let me Know how they all are

A. J. McElveen to Z. B. Oakes,
Sumterville, S.C., 9 August 1853. (196)

I will Send you on Thursday a no 1 Boy for our country   the fellow I intended to have the dogs after he came
in monday Evening.   I Bought him in the morning and
came to me in the Evening   I paid $950 for him   I Bought
him Delivered at the price but he delivered him Self.   I
hold him over in hopes to Get more to Send with him   I
will leave here on Thursday that is the 11th inst   I cant Get
Back here a Gain before the 15th or 16 inst   The desire of
his owners are Edward must leave the State if Posible though
he is not Gilty off no criminal offence but if Properly managed will be a fine Boy   do not have him punished if you
can help it   he is very Easy fritened.   he is the Best Stripped fellow I Ever Examined   Edward weighes 165 lbs   5
feet 8 inches high   Mr Oakes I want you to Get twelve Hundred Dollars for him   if any fellow 20 years old will bring
that price I think he will   if you can Sell Edward in the city
do So   his wife is there   the norton Girl molatto   perhaps Tupper[5] will Bye him.   I am not Restricted By written
a Greement to Send him out the State   The Boy is very anxious to Stay in town but do as you like   you must not let
the Boy come up this way after Sold   any person who Byes
Edward they need not confine him   he will Go with them
any where   the Boy cannot bear Punishment or Confine-
ment.   I will try and make Some arrangments a bout Selling Doss up here if I can   I have not had time to do any
thing a bout it

---

5. Probably T[ristram] Tupper and Son, Charleston commission merchants,
Brown's Wharf. Charleston city directory (1855), 106.

A. J. McElveen to Z. B. Oakes,
Sumterville, S.C., 10 August 1853. (195)

I beg you to instruct me in Bying Still.   I am offred to day a woman 25 or 28 years old   tolerable likely   Good field hand   She is well formed and Stout built   Sound and harty   her teeth a little defective   also a tolerable Good cook   washes well   also a Good Stearcher and Ironer   they are no doubt in all these qualifications.   I can bye her for $750   I think the market might afford the price.   I am offred a fellow to day for $900.   his master Says he is with in one Inch of Six feet   only 23 years old prety well propotioned   he has bad teeth   do Say if I can Stand the prices.   Excuse me for troubling you for infermation.   you may think I ought to be well Posted up but I hate to leave any thing undun and I wish at the Same time to please you in all my purcheses.   do write me By the 15th inst.   I Send you the fellow Bought of Mrs. [Pedrow?][6] the title is unquestionable   I bought 8 negros from the Same Estate last winter one year ago   I paid $950 for Edward   I want you to Get $1250 for him if Posible.   I leave here to-morrow   I think I will be absent one week from here   I will be down after Sale day in Sept   I understand they will be twelve negros Sold that day   that is on the first monday in Sept   you will here from me before that time

A. J. McElveen to Z. B. Oakes,
Sumterville, S.C., 18 August 1853. (189)

Boath yours came Safe to hand.   I arrived here yester-day Evening.   I am Sorry you did not Say anything a bout

---

6. Possibly Esther Perdriau of Sumter District. In 1860 she was described as a planter living in Privateer. See Teel, *1850 Census, Sumter-District,* dw. 639; Teel, *1860 Census, Sumter-District,* dw. 1384.

my Bying the fellow I discribed had Bad teeth Good Size   I
will See him in the morning   I have not Bought any Since
I wrote you.   if I Get the fellow in the morning I will Keep
him until monday   I have a call to See a likely Girl and I
will Send them down on monday.   you will please Send to
the R.R. monday   they are very few offring at this time
I think I will Bye the Girl as the Gentleman has Bin trying to
Sell to me Since last year.   it is Strange Robert[7] left as he
did without Saying any thing to me.   I think he might waited
until I came down   have you Sold Jack[8]   if So I dont
Know how you are to do a bout the office.   I Reced a few
lines from Robt Stating he had left for Missisippi   I will leave
here a Gain monday for Darlington and will be a bsent for
ten days   answer this By Sundays mail   I will do my best
to Get all the Stock I can by the first Sept   I Expect to be
down Immediately after Sale day that comes on 5th   can
you tell what Business Robert will be engaged at.   do let
me Know if he Said any thing to you a bout Going a way

A. J. McElveen to Z. B. Oakes,
Sumterville, S.C., 20 August 1853. (187)

yours of the 19th came Safe to hand.   I have bought
the fellow I discribed had bad teeth   the freckeled faced
Boy I droped Some time Since.   I dont think I Got avery
Good Bargain in him   he weighs only 145 lbs   5 feet 7

---

7. Possibly Robert S. Adams, an agent for the firm of Adams and Wicks
   in Aberdeen, Mississippi. That summer he also visited North Carolina,
   Virginia, and Maryland to purchase slaves. See A. J. McElveen to Z. B.
   Oakes, 10 October 1853, Oakes Papers, and note 16 below.
8. Jack, a waiting man for J. S. Riggs and Z. B. Oakes, was purchased
   from Florida. See Schwartz and Habersham to Z. B. Oakes, 6 October
   1853, A. G. Farnboro to Z. B. Oakes, 29 February 1855, Oakes Papers.

inches.   I hope you may be able to Get commissions on him   he is tollerable likely and young Enough to Sell Readly. I understand Belser has agents up here Since he was down By Seeing negros in Great demand and is offring $900 for 15 year old Boys.   I paid 9 hundred for phillip Belonging to Mr John B Brogdon[9] a man I look on as a Gentleman of Sumter and has done me a Great many favors   he would not take a Dollar less for him.   I will Send him down on Tuesday as friend Jones[10] is Going down on that day, and I want to Buy another to Send with him.   likely woman.   I will See what I can do next week a bout Selling Doss   I am Going over to See Mr McCall of Darlington   I think in my travels I will Sell him or make a Swop   I will do my best.   the Girl Emly I have yet   I came near trading her once and a nother man wants her which I have not Seen   I hope I will See him Soon.   I will try very hard to Get her off   By train I come down.   I cant well leave Before this 5 Sept. I am compeled to leave in the morning to Meet an ingagement By noon monday Some 30 miles in the lower part the district. on my way I Expect to Bye a Girl which I will Send down on Tuesday.   please write me the last of next week that is 26 or 27.   I will try and be here a gain   perhaps I will write you from Darlington C.H. if I See any thing worth Speaking a bout

9. John Bagnal Brogdon had a plantation just south of Sumterville. Teel, *1850 Census, Sumter-District*, dw. 289; Teel, *1860 Census, Sumter-District*, dw. 767; Nicholes, *Historical Sketches*, 1: 388; Cassie Nicholes, *Historical Sketches of Sumter County: Its Birth and Growth* (Sumter, S.C.: Sumter County Historical Commission, 1981), 2: 460.

10. Possibly E. H. Jones, a Sumterville merchant. Teel, *1850 Census, Sumter-District*, dw. 1822; A. J. McElveen to Z. B. Oakes, 9 September 1854, Oakes Papers.

A. J. McElveen to Z. B. Oakes, Darlington, S.C., 25 August 1853. (185)

I am here quite well   hope this will meet you and famly the Same.   nothing of much importance to write   too negros offred me to day   I have a Great mind to Bye them for I think them nearly as low as I can find any where.   the likelest Girl I Ever Saw   Black   18 years old   very near as tall as I am   no Surplus flesh   fine form   never was abused   I can Bye her for $900 no less   the boy 17 or 18 years old likely for $900   he is not as tall as the Girl if the market can Stand the Price I will come over next week and Get them   write me as Soon as you Get this.   Since writing the Gentleman came in   I Bought the Boy for $850, and I concluded to take the Girl at 900.   She weighs 173 lbs   5 feet 10 and three quarters inches high   Boath very likely   I will come over here monday after them and Send them to you on Tuesday   do Send to the cars for them the Boy will Runaway at times   he was Bough in charleston Some 4 years a Go.   it is a tall price but you Know we cant By unless we pay high   the Girl is a Good field hand   the Boy also   I hope you will be pleased with them and I think they will pay at least $100 that is 50 Each   the Girl ought to Sell for $1000.   I will be in Sumterville on Saturday in order to Get the money.   I have with me five hundred and little over   if capt William Butlers[11] negros are Sold on Sail day that is 5 Sept I will want more money   I would like you to write moses to let me have the money if I Should want it as I dont wish you to Send on an uncertainty   they are 12 negros advertised to be Sold on the 5 Sept   do dont neglect to Send to the cars on 30 inst.

---

11. Possibly W. F. Butler, planter, Sumter District. Teel, *1850 Census, Sumter-District*, dw. 567.

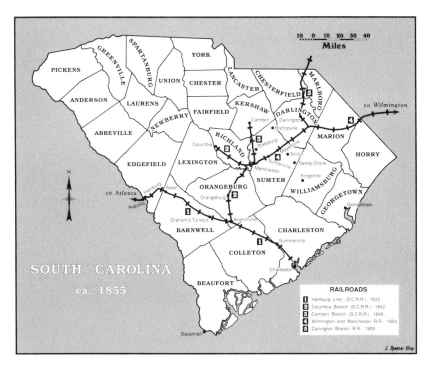

Map 1. South Carolina, ca. 1855.
(Based on "South Carolina," published by J. H. Colton & Co., No. 172 William St., New York, 1855.)

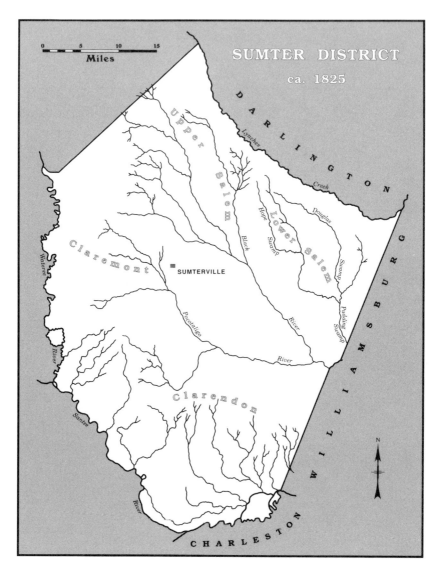

Map 2. Sumter District, ca. 1825.
(Based on "Sumter District, South Carolina," Surveyed by S. H. Boykin, 1821. Improved for Mills Atlas, 1825.)

Letter, A. J. McElveen to Z. B. Oakes, 15 May 1854. (Courtesy the Trustees of the Boston Public Library.)

Advertisement of slave purchased by A. J. McElveen for Z. B. Oakes. (Reprinted from Charleston *Mercury*, 1 February 1854.)

Charleston slave auction, northside of the Exchange, near Atlantic Wharf, 10 March 1853. (Reprinted from *Illustrated London News,* 29 November 1856.)

Sumter District Court House, where A. J. McElveen participated in slave auctions, 1893. (Reprinted from John R. Poindexter, *Sumter County: A Photographic Chronicle, 1845–1955* [Sumter, S.C.: Sumter County Museum, 1989].)

Gravestone, Z. B. Oakes, Magnolia Cemetery. (Photograph by Terry Flippo in author's possession.)

Confederate statuary, Magnolia Cemetery, Charleston. (Photograph by Terry Flippo in author's possession.)

Gravestone, Mary (Polly) Burrill, mother of Z. B. Oakes, Magnolia Cemetery. (Photograph by Terry Flippo in author's possession.)

"The Fifty-Fifth Massachusetts Colored Regiment Singing John Brown's March in the Streets of Charleston, February 21, 1865." (Reprinted from *Harper's Weekly*, 18 March 1865.)

Charles Carleton Coffin, Boston *Journal* correspondent who seized war relics from the slave mart
on Chalmers Street. (Reprinted from Coffin, *Four
Years of Fighting.*)

James Redpath, New York *Tribune* correspondent
who confiscated the letters of Z. B. Oakes. (Courtesy Kansas State Historical Society, Topeka.)

Boston Public Library, Boylston Street, ca. 1890, original depository of the Z. B. Oakes Papers, donated November 11, 1891. (Courtesy the Trustees of the Boston Public Library.)

Old Slave Mart Museum, Chalmers Street, 1990. (Photograph by Terry Flippo in author's possession.)

A. J. McElveen to Z. B. Oakes,
Darlington Court House, S.C., 29 August 1853. (182)

I Send you two negros By Rail Road.   Bill and Ann. I hope they will Reach Safe and please you, also, Suit the market.   I think them very likely and consequentely will meet Ready Sail.   I think the price very high   I trust you will make a fare profit on Them   I paid $900 for Ann and $850 for Bill   Boath Good field hands   the Boy a first Rate Plowmon.   I came over here on the cars yesterday and had ten miles to travel By Stage.   I will Return in the morning to Sumterville and Send the negros to charleston.   Emly is on trial and if the lady is pleased with her, I will Get a Boy 14 years of age likely the Brother of Betsy.   I will pay $150. between the too that will bring the Boy to $800.   if the trade is made I will Get the Boy in the morning and Send him down also.   I am looking for negros in   I am told they will be Some offred me to day   if I Get any more I will try and Send them down Immediately.   I will be down the 7th Sept
  P.S. I Saw the lady Mrs. Blackwell who wishes to Sell 4 or 5 negros   She has promised to waite until I Return from charleston before She Sells   I will leave [ ]¹²

A. J. McElveen to Z. B. Oakes,
Sumterville, S.C., 3 October 1853. (176)

I haste to drop you a line   I could not bye any thing to day   prices was very tall   the primest Boy Sold for $1105   one famly Sold for $1640 likely woman 4 children an old woman and too Boy and one Girl Sold for $2800   the four negros I thought worth a bout $2500   you See from the Sale they was no chance for me.   I bought 2 fellows on

---

12. Bottom of page is torn.

Saturday last for $2000   they was to be Sent to me to day
but has not come in yet So if they dont come in Soon I will
have to take another trip for them   I Supposes they are
Runaway   do Send to the Rail Road Every day this week
as I will have Some negros down this week.   I bought the
old cook for $450 the lowest dollar I could bye her.   I was
compeled to bye me a horse   my hose is lame So bad he
cant travel   I think I bought a cheap horse Six years old
for $135   well broke and fine axion   I hope you will not
think hard of my bying as I cant Get a bout without Some
thing to haul me   the other horse will be no Expence as I
has Sent him to my brother   please Enquire for letters for
me and Send them up   if the too fellows do not come this
Evening be ceartain to Send to cars on thursday as the cook
will come if none others

A. J. McElveen to Z. B. Oakes,

Sumterville, S.C., 6 October 1853. (175)

   I omited one notice this morning By Didry.   I Bought a
woman from Dr McCauly which I will Get on the 14th inst   I
am to pay him $800 for her   She is likely   a bout 25 years
old   never had any children   tall for a woman   Good
teeth   fine form   I will Send her down on the 15th if nothing happens to prevent.   I dont think they are any Back out
in that trade   I have Seen him Since I made the trade.   Mr
Oakes if Belser has put his negros with B Mordecai[13] do look
at the 2 he Sent on Tuesday last.   a fellow I Bought last winter from John Congess Runaway I was to pay him $700 for him
Belser Gave $1000   if they are any money to be made on
Such fellows I want to Know it Bad   do dont let on you have

---

13. Benjamin Mordecai, Charleston broker, 5 State Street. See Charleston
    city directory (1860), 5.

---

any infermation atall   he also Give over $700 for a Girl whiped very Bad   in a famly way   She is Small Size wo-man   do let me here from you Soon and please Give me your Ideas on Such Stock if you can See them   also on J. S. Ryan Boys and one Girl he Bought from Burkett.   I have wrote to Mr J. R. Stall[14] to call and See the cook   if you dont want her let Mr Stall have her at $500 as he promised to Pay me fifty Dollars profit on a Good Cook.

A. J. McElveen to Z. B. Oakes,

Sumter District, S.C., 10 October 1853. (172)[15]

this will inform you I Expect to Send a fellow down in the morning and hope he will arrive Safe.   it is very hard to Bye negros.   I must beg you to inform me the hiest Price I must Give for likely Girls a bout Such as Betsy you Sent to adams.[16] I am offred too for $900 Each   I think that is too high also I am offred too others for $1500   one a bout 30   the other 18   Both likely   one of them a firstrate cook also Good Seamstress.   the other Good field hand.   I am on

---

14. John R. Stall, of nearby Summerville, owned real estate in Charleston worth $26,900 in 1860. Stall purchased Didry, probably this cook, whom he found unsatisfactory. See A. J. McElveen to Z. B. Oakes, 27 October 1853, J. R. Stall to Z. B. Oakes, 19 February 1855, Oakes Papers; *List of the Tax Payers of the City of Charleston for 1860*, 268; Frederick A. Ford, *Census of the City of Charleston, South Carolina, for the Year 1861* (Charleston: Evans and Cogswell, 1861), 116, 125, 150.

15. Letter indicates it was sent by "S. C R R" to Oakes's office at "No 7 State Street."

16. Probably Robert S. Adams, agent, firm of Adams and Wicks, Aberdeen, Mississippi. R. S. Adams to Z. B. Oakes, 22 July, 29 July 1853, Adams and Wicks to Z. B. Oakes, 4 January 1854, Oakes Papers; Tadman, *Speculators and Slaves*, 55–56; Bancroft, *Slave-Trading in the Old South*, 309.

my way to Sumterville and waiting for the Boy I bought last week.   I am to Give $960 for him   a bout 22 years of age. I have left Doss with Mr George McCall   he is to try and Sell him for me by court that is by the 17 inst   I will be at Darlington C.H. on that day   Send to the R.R. on 15th   I will Send one or more that day   do rite me Im-mediately as I will leave Sumterville on Saturday next   I am offred one large lot of land I think cheep in Sumterville   2 and half Acres for $8000   too thousand cash and three years to Pay the Ballance   Several houses on the lot which Rents for Eleven hundred Dollars this year   if you would like to See it I will Get Get the Parties to waite until you can comeup and See it   I think the hole lot can be cut up in 12 or 15 lots and in a few years be worth three times the amount   write me what you think a bout it   the Parties will do nothing until I Say what I will do   I Expect to here from you as Soon as I Get in Sumterville   I write this on my way as I will take the cars at lynchburg.

P.S. I Send you Boy Joe   I hope he will arrive Safe do try and Get $1050 for him   I paid $960   he is all right and Smooth   Good title   right me Immediately if you please

A. J. McElveen to Z. B. Oakes,
Sumterville, S.C., 12 October 1853. (170)

I drop you a line in haste hoping it will meet you and famly well.   it leaves me well   I was very unwell yesterday. you will oblige me to Send to the R.R. on Saturday 15th   I have 2 women to Send on that day without Sickness prevents I bought one yesterday   a Girl about 15 years old   toler-able likely field hand   I am to Pay for Boath on friday $700 for the 15 year old Girl and $800 for the woman 25 years old   She is tall and likely Good field hand   Dr McCally is the owner of woman and Says an order on you will answer his purpose   if you have no objection to it I will Give him an order on you for $800   let me here from you By Return Mail as I wish to leave here on Saturday for darlington   I think I will bye Some over there court week   also I hope to dispose of Doss or make Some Exchange for others.   I think the a bove too negros will pay at least $100 profit 50 Each   if we can make Even fifty Dollars on the head at the Present rates I think we may be Satisfied

Except my Respect you and famly.

A. J. McElveen to Z. B. Oakes,
Sumterville, S.C., 14 October 1853. (169)

I Send you one negro Girl only.   I am very much diss-appointed a bout McCaly   it is Strange   it is but the fewest number of men can be depended on in our day.   I hope the Girl Darky will Reach Safely and meet Ready Sale She is a very fare Girl Sold for no fault only for the want of money   Sound and Good title   I Paid $700 for her   I think She will pay a fare profit.   Say to Mr Trumbo[17] I will inquire in to the case of Milton   I think it will turnout faults.   I will draw on you for a Small amount tomorrow. I have Concluded to take no money with me over to Darling-ton Court, as it is So hard to Bye.   I am in Great hope of

---

17. Probably Christopher Columbus Trumbo, Charleston builder and master mason. He owned ten slaves and several houses in Charleston around 1860. The section where he lived and owned a row of houses was called Trumbo's Court. Charleston city directory (1855), 106; U.S. Census, 1850, S.C., Charleston, 129; U.S. Census, 1860, S.C., Charleston, 230; *List of the Tax Payers of the City of Charleston for 1860*, 283; Ford, *Census*, 106, 139, 207; C. C. Trumbo to Z. B. Oakes, 20 May [1857?], Oakes Papers.

Bying a few over there not withstanding.   Should I Get
any there I will have them down by 21st or 22nd inst ceartain   I have entirely fagoten to acknowledge the Receipt of
your two letters, 8th and 13th inst   they was duly Recd and
contents perticularly noticed.   I hope Some of our big men
up here will be convinced in the Prices of negros.   let me
here from you Soon.

A. J. McElveen to Z. B. Oakes,

Sumterville, S.C., 22 October 1853. (168)

        yours came Safe to hand   I have Just arrived from Dar-
lington   I am very Sory I cannot Geather Stock.   you
Know I do my best and always trying to do the best I can.
you also Know, Mr Oakes I Indevour to bye Such negros that
will pay and your advise or Instructions are to bye Such that
will pay a profit if I Get but fear, the fact is I cant find negros
for Sale that will pay a profit   Mr Oakes I wish your advise
at all times.   I hope to Get Some next week   Mr Williamson told me I could have his too women at $1500.   I
have offred him $1450   a likely Girl year old 18 a Good
field hand   a likely woman 30 year old first rate cook and
Seamstress.   I discribed the Same to you last week.   I
cannot buy them at what you mentioned $1400.   I wish
you to write me Immediately and Give me all the Instructions
you can   I hope to bye too or three negros from Mr Allen[18]
on monday if I like them   young Girl 12 or 13 and her
mother 30 or 35   he ask me $1200 for them   I offred
him 1150   he then proposed to put a Small Boy in at a low
price and he ask me $1500 for the three   I will See them
on monday morning and if I like them I will take them.   I

---

18. Probably a planter from Middle Salem in Sumter District. Teel, *1850
    Census, Sumter-District*, dws. 1179, 1242, 1505.

cant here here from Williamson before Thursday   do let me
here from you on mondays mail.   I See Burkett has Just arrived from charleston   I suppose, I think him one of the
poriest a poleges for a man I Ever Saw.   you can Judge no
dependence attall in him   do let me Know what he took
down if you Saw him

A. J. McElveen to Z. B. Oakes,
Sumterville, S.C., 27 October 1853. (164)

yours came duly to hand and contents noticed.   I am
very Glad you Give me Such instructions   you See from
My Slow bying I was not anxious to take hold.   you will
be Kind Enough to Continue Giving instructions.   do let
me here from Susan   I have intirely neglected Enquirerys
after her.   I leave here in the morning and will be Back a
Gain the 5th november   I Send you the letter Giving infermation a bout milton which I hope will Give all Satisfaction
in regard to his faults assersions   as for old Didry tell Mr
Stall, Mr Solomons[19] Says if he lets the old woman a lone She
will allways lie up.   She is no more Sickly than women are
Generally.   Mr Oakes I Say dont take her Back unless he
has her Examind by a Doctor you appove off and find Something are Rong with her, I am Sory to State and you Know
best what to do.   dont be Bothered So much with Such
falts [tailes] from negroes   when men Bys negros tell them
to Call in a Doct if they cant believe me and yourself   I
dont deceive no man if I an awise of the fact.   When I Return to Sumterville I will Send you the order for the Girl I Sold
up here   I hope Doss will Return Safe   I cant Do any

---

19. Perhaps one of the Solomons brothers, two Sumterville merchants. See
    Teel, *1850 Census, Sumter-District*, dw. 1849; Teel, *1860 Census, Sumter-*
    District, dw. [1463?] (2).

thing with him up here   do try and Get cost for him if Posibly   I am very Sory to Say I am in Some trouble for Several days past.   one of my nephews got Shot dead Some ten days a go, Simpley from Keeping company with bad men. I will tell you when I See you all a bout it   Mr Oakes I would be glad if you could come up Sail day that is the 7th nov.   they will be Some negros offred that day and I am told likely ones   the 7th is the commencement of our Court it is very healthy up here.   we had white frost which I think has Killed vegatation.

P.S. I will Send the Recipt that will Show to you and Mr Cottall I have a warrantee as to Soundness   also title   do look for our friend [Mr.?] W. Benbow who deceived me in too fellows   he has taken too down for Sale   the primest one is the one I Bought   the Inferior one I dont Know Skin him if you can

A. J. McElveen to Z. B. Oakes,

Kingstree, Williamsburg District, S.C., 2 November 1853. (158)

I am at a lost to Know what to do negros offring   Every day I hope Some change will take place Soon   the Business Season on hand and nothing doing atall   do let me Know on Recipt of this note what I must do   if I cant do nothing here I had as well come down and assist you if I can.   I never wish to be Idle as long as I am able to Get a bout.   I hope you will be able to meet me in Sumterville on the 7th if you dont meet me or let me here from you I will be perfectly at a lost if any thing offres   do inform me how the markets Ranges   if the Best fellows can Stand $900, and women $700.   if this Reaches you in time and you cannot come up do let me here from you By Sunday Evening mail

McElveen Letters [1853]

A. J. McElveen to Z. B. Oakes,
Sumterville, S.C., 7 November 1853. (156)[20]

yours came Safe to hand yesterday   I was Glad to here from you.   I have Bought 2 negroes to day at private Sale. ten head Sold at public out cry.   I could not touch.   the fact is the most was Bought in.   the Small Boy [Primus?] cost me $600   the fellow will $850.   Send to the Rail Road for them on wednesday   the Boys will not please you in Every Respect   the fellow has a Soar leg but can be cuard very Soon   do Get Save that will heal it.   I had him Examined By Dr Ingram.   he advises his owner Mr Mcleod[21] to warrant him Sound   the little Boy has one of his toes cut off.   I dont think that will lessen his value

I hope you will make fify on Each   I think they are worth that at least   the fellow may appear Simple but he is Got as Good Sense as the most of negros   Doct Ingram has Known the Boy for a length of time and Says he never Gives him medicine but once for Belly Ache   he is Smaller than I like but it is hard to Buy at any price up here   let me here from you on the arrival of the negros

A. J. McElveen to Z. B. Oakes,
Sumterville, S.C., 8 November 1853. (155)

I Send you two negros *will & primus*   I hope they will please you better than you Expected   also I hope you will

---

20. Mailing instructions *"In haste"* are written on back of letter.
21. McElveen bought Will and Primus from Napoleon McLeod and perhaps from his brother Robert. Dr. John I. Ingram assured McElveen that the sore on Will's leg was not serious. Oakes, however, refused to accept the slave and the McLeods agreed to take him back. See certificate by J. I. Ingram, 8 November 1853, A. J. McElveen to Z. B. Oakes, 8 November, 13 November, 9 December 1853, Oakes Papers.

Excuse me buying Such.   I trust you will make a fare Profit on them.   I Send you Dr Ingram certificate, hoping that will Give more Satisfaction   will $850.   Primus $600. I am offred a woman 27 years old   a first Rate cook   tolerable Good teeth   low   tolerable well bilt   fair looking   clear of marks   the price are $700 an She worth it or not   perhaps I can Get her at $650   will She pay at $700   please let me Know By Return mail

A. J. McElveen to Z. B. Oakes,
Sumterville, S.C., 9 November 1853. (152)

Inclosed I Send you an order on Messrs Reeder & Dessaussure[22] from Mr Mcfadden[23] for the Girl Emly which are Due us on the Sale of Said negro Girl.   you will please collect.   Mr Reeder told me he would Except it   also this will inform you I have purchased three negros to day   I will Send them to you on 14th inst   they will be delivered to me on Saturday the 12th and I will Send them down on monday   do let me here from you on Receipt of this

A. J. McElveen to Z. B. Oakes,
Sumterville, S.C., 13 November 1853. (146)

Boath of your letters came Safe to hand.   I am Extremely Sorry   indced I was So blinded in the Boy will I am at a lost to Know what to Resort to in Such a case.   I bought him openly and Mr Mcleods physician Present at the

22. Reeder and DeSaussure were Charleston factors and commission merchants, Adger's Wharf. See Sumter *Watchman*, 7 November 1855.
23. In 1850 there were at least eight planters in Sumter District surnamed McFaddin (also spelled "McFadden"). The McFaddens were early pioneers. Teel, *1850 Census, Sumter-District*, dws. 260, 433, 1586, 1657, 1693, 1694, 1695; Revill, *Sumter District*, 23.

time.   you must advise me what I will do   I cannot loose money that way.   I leave here in the morning and cannot Get Back before Saturday the 19th.   if you think best Send the Boy back on Saturday at which time I will meet him at the R.R depot in Sumterville and do as you direct me.

I Send you 3 negros to wit, Betty & her daughter Fanny & her Son Abram   the Boy is not warranted Sound boath the others are warranted Sound.   I dont think they are very high at $1500.   I think they will pay a fare profit though I may be deceived   the woman is a first rate cook or field hand   the Girl is a Smart house Girl.   the Boy is also Smart waiting Boy   I am willing for any body to try them.   also, the Boy will finely Recover from his diseases if Properly treated.   that is Dr W S. Burgess opinion as he is bin under his treatment for Some time Past

Mr Oakes I hope you will not be displeased with this lot of negros   as you Know I wish to please you in Every Respect, and if the market is in Such a low or deprest condition and money cant be made on Such Stock do let me Know and I will be ceartain to mend my ways in Buying here after.   I wish to make one propersition, I am offred 13 negros and lot in Sumterville for ten thousand Dollars one third cash. prety fine house on it   Six acres land   I will Get a list of the negros in the morning and perhaps See them.   one woman 50 [12?]24 from 26, down to 6 years old, only 4 under ten years old   they are 4 fellows I am told worth $1000 Each.   after I See them and view the place over I will Give you a full Statement of the matter, and futher if you wish to Back me please let me Know.   I feel it my duty to Give you the Refusal at all times.   Should I feel disposed to make the trad I will let you Know   they are a Gentleman in our vi-

---

24. [12?] is written in superscript after "50."

cinity has 14 negros which he will put in market a bout January, and Puting the hole lot together of 27 will be worth while the trouble   I have no doubt the place can be Sold Readly   it would do prety well for a county Resort for your famly.

A. J. McElveen to Z. B. Oakes,
Sumterville, S.C., 9 December 1853. (134)[25]

This will inform you I arrived here Safe with the Boy. I Returned him on yesterday.   Just as I Expected I Reced no money, only notes which I can turn in money Soon I hope I had them well Secord, adding the Intrust from the day I paid him the money   also adding the Expenses of the Boy in the notes & drawing intrust from yesterday up to Payment.   one note on J. J. Congess for $300, due Jan. 1854.   one note on McLeod and his Brother Robert L. McLeod for $565 30/100 due four months after note.   I hope I will have Some chance to turn the notes in another negro Soon   they have promised to assist me in doing So   I believe I am Safe at last and I think it Better So than a law Suit.   they Regreted the thing very much and found out it would injure them if I was not made Safe.   after all I called on Dr Ingram and he advised them to Settle at all hassards without law Suit   the Reason I called on there Doctor was this they depending on his opinion, and having his advise through me would bring them to a Settlement.   I hope time will Bring all the matter to a close amicably without any further Expenses or Truble. I hope you will Concur with me in the arrangements of the matter and think it bst So than worst.

Mr Oakes I Send you three advertisements which will Sat-

---

25. Letter was written on Congress Care Company stationery. Back of letter indicates it was sent by way of "Servants *on S. Co R R.*"

isfy you   they will be Great many negros offred this winter
up here.   in maj crawfords Sale prehaps   C B Eagerton[26] is one of the creditors and he may be in charleston   if
So you may make Some arrangements with him.   if you do
let me Know and I will meet him at the Sale and assume his
claims or Send me a Power to do So.   I would like for you
to Send me three thousand Dollars a bout christmast.   I
think they will be Some chance for me to Buy at Sparks Sale.
I intend to Buy if I can See any money in negros this winter
do let me Know if they are any change in the market for better
or worst Since I left and what you think of the market after
Jan.

   my Respects to you and famly   let me Know how Susan
are Getting on

A. J. McElveen to Z. B. Oakes,
Sumterville, S.C., 13 December 1853. (129)

   you will please answer my last weeks letter and let me
Know the State of the market   I am at a lost to Know what
to Give for negros.   plenty offring high as usual   prehaps I had better not Buy before Jan.   can you Send me
the amount I wished the last of the month, or had I better Bye
first.   I wrote you the Particulars of the Boy will.   I
Returned him and took Good paper   was the Best could be
done.   it was that or nothing at the Present   I hope I
will be able to turn it in money Soon.   Mr Oakes do be
Kind Enough to let me Know what Burkett Got for the too
Boys he Carried down to charleston last week.   I dont
think he made any money on them   he paid for Each $875
that was $1750   I cant See how a man can make money at

---

26. Possibly C. B. Eagerton, farmer, Marion District. U.S. Census, 1860,
   S.C., Marion, 31.

Such Prices.   he Sold them ceartain at Some Price   I
leave here in the morning for Darlington C.H.   I will be
here the first of next week.

A. J. McElveen to Z. B. Oakes,
Sumterville, S.C., 27 December 1853. (120)

    I would be Glad to here from you   about this time I
here they are a Great deal of Smallpox in the city.[27]   are
they any danger Sending negros down, or coming my Self.
will you be up on monday to the Sale.   [Gillchrist?] came
up this Evening.   if you wish whitesides to leave on account of the Smallpox Send him up here   he can Get Board
at $12.00 per month and perhaps less.   I will be at Est L
Whites[28] tomorrow   one hundred negros will be Sold.
I dont think I will buy.   I wont to Buy on monday, as the
likelest negros will be offred that day   write on Receipt of
this

A. J. McElveen to Z. B. Oakes,
Sumterville, S.C., 2 January 1854. (116)

    I Send you a list of one lot of negroes Sold at prices I can-
not conceive why they Sold for Such, at the Present State of

---

27. In late December 1853 a smallpox scare began to shake the city. Con-
cern was such that a committee of the South Carolina Medical Association, meeting in Charleston, issued a report on the disease. By late
January 1854 sixty-four cases and eleven deaths were reported. Charles-
tonians resented the "great hue and cry" making their city appear as
"one vast charnel house" and causing "country merchants" to hurry to
New York City for "their Spring supplies." Charleston *Daily Courier,*
23, 25, 30, 31 January, 1, 2, 8, 10, 15 February 1854.

28. Possibly Sumter District planter, Leonard White, who was born in
1784. Montgomery Moses and he helped bring the railroads to Sumter
District. Teel, *1850 Census, Sumter-District,* dw. 1911; Gregorie, *History of Sumter County,* 165, 191, 541.

things.   the first lot 55, average near $600   the Second lot 53 [" " "]29   the first lot is the list I Send you   all very ordenary negroes.   I hardly Know where to Stear my course   however I will look at too lots of negros which are offred me at private Sale   Some 20 in Each lot   it is very unceartain a bout my Buying.   look for me next week whether I buy or not   Every body is in high Spirits a bout the high prices of negros, and I am fearful Some will be Deceived if negroes do not Rise in charleston   Gillchrist bout Some.   also belser Bought pretty largely.   I could not buy   therefore I looked on and made a bid occaisionally please let me here from you on Recipt of this.   let me Know how the Small pox are prevaling   if they are any danger coming down

A. J. McElveen to Z. B. Oakes,
Sumterville, S.C., 19 January 1854. (97)

I have bought the boy Isaac for $1100   I think him very prime   his Equals cannot be found in capacity.   he is a General house Servant   a Splendid carriage driver. he is also a fine painter varnisher and the Boy Says he can make a fine pannel door   he is a Genious, and its Strange to Say I think he is Smarter than I am.   also he performs well on the violin and other musical instruments.   Give him a fair trial and if you do not Get $1500 for him I am very much mistaken.   his master Says he is a first Rate cook that is meats   *I am not Restricted* to have him Sent out *the State unless I* choose.   I am under promise to not let him come back to Sumter District   therefore Sell him in charleston if you can.   I paid one half cash   the other I pay the 6 Feby   that is our Sale day.   I leave here to morrow and will be here the last of next week.   write me on the arrival

---

29. Ditto marks indicate "average near $600" for second lot as well.

of Isaac and Say what you think of him, as No. 1 fellow   I
Expect to buy Some negros down below & Several is to be
Sold here on the 6th feby   if I buy I will put off Paying as
long as I can.   I will draw Small amount to morrow in
order to meet my arrangements   if I Should buy more negros
than I can Get money to pay for I will come down a bout
febarary without you make arrangements with the bank.   I
will write you from Kingstree.   a Sale takes place on the
26 inst and they will be 5 negroes Sold.   I will tell you
J. M. E [Sharpe?] offred $1200 for Isaac and Expected to Get
him but the Doctor wished him out of Jail   he would not
take any less for him and he was a bout Sending the Boy to
Robinson & Call[30] to Sell for him.   I hope you will Get fine
price for him.

the Dr will Give me a Certificate as regards his capa-
city.   he has owned him from a child up   he is 28 years
old   a bout 5 feet 10 in.   weighs 150 lbs or 160.   fine
[Legs?]   a little whiped.   the Doct is Ready to Give any
man his opinion and will Say Every thing in his favour he
can   the Boy was lead of By mean persons caused him to
Steel.   perhaps I have Said more than is necessary.

A. J. McElveen to Z. B. Oakes,
Sumterville, S.C., 27 January 1854. (92)

on my arrival I Reced yours of 20th inst   I am Sorry
I have not bought.   I have bin trying very hard Since I Sent
Isaac   the Prices is So very high I hardely Know what to
do.   I was offred three negros for $2700.   namly a fellow
22 likely Good teeth, weighing a bout 150 lbs 5 feet 6 or 7 in

---

30. Probably Robinson, Caldwell and Company, Charleston commission
    merchants, North Atlantic Wharf. Charleston city directory (1855), 18,
    90–91.

high   a boy 15 or 16 likely weighing a bout 80 or 90 lbs.
a likely Girl 19 years old   I could not Get them any lower.
are they worth nine hundred Eeach or can any thing be made
on them at that Price   if you Say buy them I will do So.
though they are 50 miles off I dont think they will be Sold before I can Get back   please let me Know by Return mail.
I will do my best to Get Some the insuing week.   I am Still
cleare of the Small pox.

A. J. McElveen to Z. B. Oakes,
Sumterville, S.C., 31 January 1854. (93)

yours came Safe to hand   I would be Glad if you would
make arrangements with Mr Furman.   I have bought 2
negros   a fellow & Girl $1725   you Spoke of making ar-
rangements with the Bank   I Expect to Get Several negros
on Sale day and if I do my Present Letter of credid will Exaust
and I will hate to be left wanting   if you think they are any
danger Sending negros to charleston do let me Know and I will
take them to Lowerys T.O.[31] So you can Get them at any time
you wish.   I See 60 head Sent to orleans By the Davises[32]
to day at high Prices   all very likely.   negros Still Sell
high here   I will not Send until I here from you.   the
negros I bought will not be delivered until next week   Give
Susan & all my Respects.

31. Lowry's Turnout was a station on "the old Stagecoach road from Charles-
    ton to Augusta." After Seed Bamberg bought the station, it became
    known as Bamberg. Neuffer, *Names in South Carolina*, 144.
32. Possibly Richmond slave traders. Richmond city directories (1852, 1860),
    as cited in Manuscripts, Box 11, Negro and Slavery Notes, etc., pp. A95,
    A96, A96A, A97AA, Frederic Bancroft Papers.

A. J. McElveen to Z. B. Oakes,
Sumterville, S.C., 6 February 1854. (85)

I purchased 3 negros at high prices but I hope you will be able to Get cost for them and Expences   Sam $900. Susy & daughter $1205   Sam I paid only half Cash   the woman & her daughter I have one and too years credit   I think they are likely.   Sam yellow Boy 16   the woman 22 Stout   the little Girl 8 years old   I look for a fellow in the morning if he dont Runaway   I am to Pay $925 for him.   I bought one fellow to day for $1000   will Get him not before next Saturday   look for them down on wednesday.   I culd not Send them to morrow on account of trying to buy the womans husband, and I wished to See if the fellow came according to promise.   all the negros Sold very high to day.   I think if they was any bargains I Got them in the felo I bought.   So dont Sell under cost and as much over as posible.   also please have my negroes vaxinated on arrival.   be Sure to Send to Rail Road

A. J. McElveen to Z. B. Oakes,
Sumterville, S.C., 7 February 1854. (88)

I Send you 4 negroes namely Henry Sam Susanna & Tener   I hope you may do well with Them.   henry $925 Sam $900   Susanna and Tener $1205.   I want $1000 for Sam.[33]   I refused $80 profit on Sam to day.   if you cant Get one thousand for Sam please Keep him until I come down. I have a notion to take a trip to Georgia this Spring & I want a waitingman   Should I Go that dependes on our busi-

---

33. Sam was sold, but a question arose over whether or not he had trouble with sore legs. He was eventually returned to his previous owner, Mr. Blackwell, after a settlement was reached. A. J. McElveen to Z. B. Oakes, 6 July, 17 July 1854, Oakes Papers.

ness.   Sam is likely and Smart waiting boy no mistake
Sold for no fault   the negros are all Sound & helthy I believe.   the woman will complain but She is unwilling to
leave   I think She will need correcting.   I could not buy
her husband   do try and Get $1300 for the woman &
daughter   henry is prime field hand, and very active fellow
he wish to be Sold in charleston.   I am fearful he will Give
you the Slip if you Give him any chance.   the boy I bar-
gained for at $1,000 to be deliverd next Saturday is one hun-
dred dollars beter than henry.   do let me here what you
think of the Present Prices Know & for the future.   if you
See any danger negroes are likely to come down you will
please not hold on.   Sell all.

did White[34] call to See the Blacksmith   he wrote me
he would meet me in charleston at the Races[35]

My Respects to Susan & all the famly   how do the
Small pox prevaile.

A. J. McElveen to Z. B. Oakes,
Sumterville, S.C., 11 February 1854. (74)

yours came to hand this afternoon   also yours of the
ninth.   I am very Sorry things turnout So badly.   the

---

34. Probably G. W. White. The slave blacksmith could be Doss.
35. Dating back to 1734, Charleston's "Race Week" was held annually during February. Sponsored by the South Carolina Jockey Club, it con-
sisted of four days of racing at the Washington Race Course and a
grand ball. Purses totaled in the thousands of dollars. Courts, schools,
and most business establishments were closed. "Race Week" provided
planters an excellent opportunity to both socialize and do business. It
was not unusual for the South Carolina Medical Association to hold
its annual meeting in Charleston around that time. Robert P. Stockton,
"Race Week Highlighted Pre-Civil War Era," Charleston *News and
Courier*, 25 June 1973, 1B. Charleston *Daily Courier*, 26, 27, 30 January,
1, 2, 3, 4, 6 February 1854, 6, 7 February 1855, 6 February 1857.

boy henry has a wide Range up here and I cant Say how long it will take me to have him apprehended.   I will notify his master and endevour to have him picked up if he Should Get him Safe   I am very Sory indeed.   I cannot Get better negros or Such that will Sell Readly.   I am Sure I do the Best I can for our intrust and all ways have done So.   I cant come down before the first of march and Should Henry be taken to you please have him placed in the work house[36]

I am well and hope this will meet you all the Same.

{Please Except my Draft drawn today}

A. J. McElveen to Z. B. Oakes,
Sumterville, S.C., 6 March 1854. (61)

I Send you an order on Mr J S Riggs for too hundred & Six dollars which I wish you to collect and place the Same to my credit.   Mr Jones left a negro in the hands of Mr Riggs for Sale   I bought one fellow to day for $1025   it is too high but I Got off one of the notes in part payment on Mcleod for $575.   I also paid on the Boy will Sold to Briscoe $247. that is the amount of Draft I drawn to day.   the Boy is prime 24 years old.   a bout 5 feet 9 inches   weighs a bout 160 lbs.   I was offred $1100 for him to day but I promised his owner that is Mr W. Fort to Send him out of the State   nothing much a Gainst him but Mr fort wishes him Sent to the west, if posible.   he will Runaway if you Give him the least chance.   I cant Sell henry I dont think & I will Send them boath down the last of the week, as Soon as the trusle are replaced in the Swamp.

---

36. Work houses were places where slaves were disciplined and temporarily housed. In 1855 Charleston had two, one for the upper wards and another for the lower wards. Charleston city directory (1855), appendix, 5.

Mr W. H. McKnight[37] who Left a negro in your hands for Sale begd me to Say to you to authurise me to pay him the amount of ($500) five hundred Dollars   he told me you promised to Send him Some money by me.   I Said to him I Supposed the Reson why I came down Sooner than you Expected.   if you wish I will pay him the money over as Soon as I Can here from you.   please let me here from you Immediately   I may come down the last of the week.   Mr McKnight is in Great need of money to pay out the Sherieffs office.

A. J. McElveen to Z. B. Oakes,
Sumterville, S.C., [8?] March 1854. (58)

I Send the two fellows henry & bob By Mr Burgham   I Suppose you Know the cost.   I Suppose I Give more than Bob was worth   the Reason I Gave the price, I Got cleare of one note   perhaps I might bin Kept out the money twelve months, & Such men and notes I wish to Keep cleare off.   I hope you will do well with the too boys   they are boath Runaways & I want them Sent out off the State if Posible. you will please have them placed in the work house.   Mr Oakes I dont wish any person to Know what I pay for negros Except my self and you.   if they cant Give the Price you think proper persons can let them alone.   I dont intend to buy without   I can Get them much lower than I have bin buying.   do you wish me to come down and Stay a while or do you think I can do much by taking a trip up the country. please let me here from you on Recept of this.   I Expected to here from you this Evening, in answer to mine Last monday

---

37. Sumter District planter living near Wright's Bluff. Sumter (Sumterville) *Black River Watchman*, 10 February 1854; Teel, *1850 Census, Sumter-District*, dw. 180.

A. J. McElveen to Z. B. Oakes,
Sumterville, S.C., 13 March 1854. (53)[38]

Yours of the 10th & 12th came duly to hand

I Send you Mr McKnight Recipt for (.$505.) five hundred & five Dollars advance on boy Ely.   he pays the thirty days Intrust.   also I drawn Some my Self in order to pay Some Expences due.   please charge me for the Same.   I Recd a note from Mr Wilson[39] of Darlington   he wishes to buy henry or make Exchange.   I will call on Mr Wilson to morrow.   if you have not Sold him do waite until I See wilson.   Il let you here from me by thirsdays' mail.   Mr Oakes as regards my notions a bout the price I pay for negros being Known I did not mean any thing to take Exceptions at.   therefore I hope you will not think further a bout it. I think persons are believing negros will be lower.   let me here from Susan & all the Famly.

A. J. McElveen to Z. B. Oakes,
Darlington, S.C., 15 March 1854. (54)

this will inform you I have done the Best I can to Sell Henry.   I am offred $1000 on the first of Oct next, clear of interest   wilson will Give an order on W. K. Ryan the factor.   to be Excepted he Says.   Ryan will Except.   I dont Know how that will Suite you.   you Know Ryan and I Know him also.   I Know wilson to be Responsable.   you Know whither Mr Ryan is or not.   if the arrangement Suits you.   if not we can only drop it   I cant Give the prices

---

38. "Robert [I I. Sumter?]," written on upper left corner of letter, perhaps refers to Robert Heriot, a Sumter District planter. See A. J. McElveen to Z. B. Oakes, 1 May 1854, Oakes Papers, and annotation on Herriot.

39. S. B. Wilson in A. J. McElveen to Z. B. Oakes, 15 March 1854, Oakes Papers.

for his negros   they are Several wilsons a bout here   this
is S. B. Wilson.   you can See Mr Ryan if you wish to make
Such arrangements, and let me Know By Return mail

A. J. McElveen to Z. B. Oakes,
Darlington, S.C., 22 March 1854. (57)

Since I wrote by yesterdays mail, Mr Wilson tells me Mr
Ryan is not willing to indorse his paper payable as Early as
oct, as he is not ceartin Mr wilson will have cotton to meet
the demands.   as regardes that you need not be uneasy.
Mr W. is Good and can Give Good Surety up here, if you can
be Satisfied with the arrangement.   I drop this through Mr
Epperson as he is traveling through.   if you can do better
with henry, it is all Right.   I Know you are Satisfied what
is best to do in the matter.   I am fearful Henry is a hard
case Since negros are on the decline

please let me here from you as Early as posible   no
chance to buy up here.

A. J. McElveen to Z. B. Oakes,
Sumterville, S.C., 3 April 1854. (42)

yours was duly Recd.   the Sale to day was very high
as usal.   I could not touch with ten feet pole.   the Sale
for Cash was very pore.   no title could be had to rely on.
however I bought one fellow I think low $750   20 years
old   weigh 150.   teeth not very Good   near my height.
I Expect to buy too tomorrow.   I think I will be down the
midle of the week.   if I dont come I will Send the fellow
& the Boy & Girl, if I buy them on thursday.   I also will
Get a Single Girl as Soon as I can See her.   I have the
promise of one for $700   young & prety likely.   I will
try and See her wednesday & bring or Send all on thursday.

my Respects to all the famly   nothing new

A. J. McElveen to Z. B. Oakes,
Sumterville, S.C., 14 April 1854. (48)

I Recd' a note from Wilson in relation to henry.   he Says he cannot buy him now, but if I will bring him over he will trade me a nother for him.   it is hard to tell what can be done in this case, but if you are disposed to Send him up I will do the best I can.   that is ceartain.   I could not buy any thing this weeke   So far the prices are too high. if you think proper to Send Henry up please pay his passage to Sumterville.   that will take a bout $2.50.C. and also Give the boy a ticket to call on Mr T. Norton[40] to remain until call for.   they are no danger of the boy Runing a way if Sent back.   if you will Send him up please Send him on monday 17 inst   I will have Some one there to meet him at depot.   I am offred $7000 worth of R.R. Stock.   I dont Know what it is worth.   I leave here tomorrow for Kingstree.   I Suppose I will be absent Some ten days without I buy.   I will write you from Kingstree

A. J. McElveen to Z. B. Oakes,
Sumterville, S.C., 21 April 1854. (33)

yours came duly to hand.   I am Sory the market is So dull.   it is dull up here.   I have just Returned from below.   they was nothing of intrust to write from Kingstree. I would be Glad if you think best Send Henry Soon, as it may be a dificult matter to get him offat any price.   do Send him up on Monday if you think it advisable   I will be here until then.   I want to look at too or three negros that is offred me next week   I am very Sory to here of the Great lost

---

40. Perhaps Timothy Norton, Sumterville wheelwright. Teel, *1850 Census, Sumter-District*, dw. 1901.

by fire in charleston.[41]   I hope the insurance will cover the Greater portion of the lost   as regards the old woman Mr Oakes She has bin Sold to long for to be returned   they are no chance for redress here.   you Know the nature of the case best, but to leave it to me I would not take her back atall   the old carpenter *John Ramsey* has runaway and placed in jail.   Sold here last Sail day for $155.   is it worth while to buy him at any price   you thought I ought to bought him when Sold   please write soon.

A. J. McElveen to Z. B. Oakes,
Sumterville, S.C., 24 April 1854. (45)

I wrote you on the 21st inst in answer to yours of the 18th   I was in hopes of hearing from you this Evening   I would be glad to Know your Ideas a bout henry   it will be too late to do any thing with him up here Soon.   I Refused a boy 19 years old to day at $800   he was tolerable likely but dull in his talking, very low in Stature for his age.   I would be Glad also if you would Give me Some quotations to be governed by as regards prices   I am at a lost at this Season.   I hope to here from you on tomorrows mail.   I will be absent the Remainder of the week.   Sail day comes on next monday.   do let me here from you this week.   the Rev J. R. pickett[42] who I Know resides in newbery Dist, Says

---

41. Early Tuesday morning, 18 April 1854, a "Destructive Fire," originating at Dr. P. M. Cohen and Company's Drug and Chemical Store on Hayne Street, spread through Market Street. Several businesses, including the dry goods establishment of the father-in-law of Oakes's daughter, were heavily damaged. Estimated fire loss was at almost a half million dollars. Charleston *Daily Courier*, 19 April, 20 April 1854.

42. Most likely John R. Pickett, Methodist minister, Newberry District. Thomas H. Pope, *The History of Newberry County, South Carolina* (Columbia: University of South Carolina Press, 1973), 1: 238.

he has three or four houses in the city and lots he is anxious to Sell them near line St.   they are in the hands of Mr Purse[43] for Sale.   he was in our town Shorte time Since. perhaps you may Get prety Good bargains in them.   Rail Road Stock is worth here $75 pr $100.   this is what I am told.   I have not witnessed any Sale here to that Effect. I Got my infermation from Good authority.   Therefore I believe it correct.

My Respects to all the famly

A. J. McElveen to Z. B. Oakes,

Sumterville, S.C., 1 May 1854. (25)

your letters was duly Recd   it is a hard matter to buy negros at any price   8 head Sold to day   2 fellows Sold for $1850.   one Girl 750   one boy 635   one famly of 4 Sold for 1445.   I dont See any chance to buy at Such prices.   Some 4 out the lot was likely & young.   they was from one year old to 50.   one fellow a bout 50   old woman a bout the Same age.   as regards burketts fellow he is the boy I wrote you about.   he is not over 5 feet 6 inch high.   will not weigh over 135 lbs.   burkett Says I can have him for $800   I think he is pretty well Sold at $750.   I dont See I have lost any thing by not buying from what you write me.   I hope the market will be better than what is anticipated at Present.   Henry came Safe.   I have not Seen him   I came in town this morning and have bin busy all day and bought nothing yet.   I dont See any chance to day to make any trade.   I offred $775 for a likely Girl in fact the likelest one I have Seen for her age this year.

---

43. Possibly Thomas F. Purse, Charleston broker who died in March 1855. Charleston *Daily Courier*, 30 March, 6 April 1854; Charleston County Death Records.

She is fine Sise   fine teeth   fine form   accustomed to house work

Mr Herriot[44] ask $900 for her.   I am ceartain that is too high   could I Stand $800.   She is only 16 years old. do write me on Recipt of this.   I will do the best I can with henry.   I will take him on to wilson as Soon as I can.   I would like to here from you before I leave for Darlington. if you think bst I will buy burketts boy at $800 if he dont leave here before I here from you   he Speaks of leaving here in the morning for hamburg.   I hope you will let me here from Susan as Soon as you can   Give my Respects to all

Excuse bad scribe as my pen was bad in the commencement

A. J. McElveen to Z. B. Oakes,

Sumterville, S.C., 3 May 1854. (24)

yours came duly to hand this afternoon.   I dont See any money in Burketts boy   he is too low   only 5 feet 2 in   145 lbs all in a bulk   he is not intelligent, and further he is not Entirely cleare of disease.   I think times is two critical to take the chance.   the Girl cannot be bought for 775 nor at 800 at this time.   Mr Herriot will Give me the refusal of her if he Sells at any price.   I have Sent Henry to wilson this Evening.   could not well Go my Self before next monday.   I am not the least affraid him runing a way while up here.   I have had him at work in order to Save Expeneses.   Should it happen So that I Send him back he will Know nothing about it.

you will please let me here from you the last of this week, any how by Sundays mail   I will be in Darlington all next

---

44. Perhaps a Sumter District planter. The name is also spelled "Heriot." See Teel, *1850 Census, Sumter-District*, dws. 1392, 1803.

week.   I will be compeled to draw on you in a day or two
if I dont buy Enough to pay Expences.

A. J. McElveen to Z. B. Oakes,
Darlington Court House, S.C., 10 May 1854. (21)

I have not made any Sale of henry yet.   I have bin
offred another boy for him and one hundred Dollars.   the
boy offred me is about 16 years of age   very likely   has
Good Sense   fine teeth but talkes badly, has impediment in
his Speech.   he talkes well to negros but cant Speake well
to white persons.   he will weigh a bout 130 lbs.   a bout
5 feet 5 or 6 inches high   I am at a lost to deside in Such
a case.   I am fearful the boy will not Sell well on account
of his Speech.   do write me on Recipt of this what you
think of the trade   I offred to trade for too hundred Dollars.
I will leave henry for a Short time   he is not on any Expences.   I will be in Sumterville the last of This week.   I
think of coming down the last of June to Spend the Summer
I will bring Henry back if I cant do any thing with him here
after the Expiration of that time.   I here of nothing offring.   let me Know the State of the market.

A. J. McElveen to Z. B. Oakes,
Sumterville, S.C., 13 May 1854. (19)

your letters came duly to hand.   I have Just come in
this morning.   in relation to Burkett, he will not do to rely
on.   as regards the case of Joe bought of Dr McRae, I can
only Say at present I will make it my business to call on him
and have the matter investigated fully, and Send his Surtifi-
cate.   the fact is the boy has told lies & you will See it as
Soon as I See the parties.

are ther any young women with one child in markets   I

can Get a prime young fellow for Such in Exchange.   I hope you have Recd my note from Darlington.   please write me by mondays mail next, as I will leave to See McRae in a few days.   I would like to here from you before I leave.   the Dr lives Some 40 m below.   I have a call Since commence writing to See a young fellow   from the message I believe I can buy him right   please Send to R.R on Tuesday.   if I buy him I will Send him down 16 inst.

A. J. McElveen to Z. B. Oakes,
Sumterville, S.C., 15 May 1854. (18)

I Send you a fellow cost $800.   I paid $200 in Slow paper[45]   I also drawn $75 for back Expences &c   the fellow named [May?]   25 years old   5 feet 7 or 8 in high.   145 lbs   bad teeth   a little whipt   I may get a Girl on the way.   I have the promise of one.   I hope the boy will do tolerable well at that price though I think it full high, and would not give it had I not Got of the Slow paper.   I will See the boy to the columbia Road   dont allow him any liberties.   I dont think he will Runaway he is very Easily managed.   as regards the Girl if I Get her please Keep her close until I write you by mail all the particulars.   She will cost $700.   pretty likely.   Mr Oakes you will please not make any Settlement a bout the boy Joe until I See Dr Mcrae   I will leave here on wednesday 17th with the intention to call on him to have the matter Settled I hope Mr McKay[46] will not think for a moment I wished to cheat him   I never wish to deceive any man

---

45. Slow paper is probably a note payable over a long period. Stephenson, *Isaac Franklin*, 59, 63.
46. Probably A. N. McKay.

A. J. McElveen to Z. B. Oakes,
Sumterville, S.C., 16 May 1854. (16)

yours came Safe to hand this afternoon. I am Sory to think we have Such trouble with the negros I purchase. I hope you will not take Joe back until I See Dr. McRae and have the matter fully investigated I am bound to hold McRae Responsible for the amount I paid that was $960 and he told me he Gave $900 and I believe him. the fact is I think if Mr McKay Gets any Redress it most be done in the *court house*, for I am fully perswaided in mind Dr McRae can produce as Respectable testimony in court as Mr McKay can. I never have heard any thing a gainst the man Since he Graduated. I am under the necessity of waiting here Some too days longer to See Mr. Norton from charleston I have assisted in Selling his lands here and he will be here on thursday morning from cheraw to have the lands Surveyed. Mr. N. promised me commissions to Sell, when I was in charleston last. the lands are Sold at $20 pr acre, the Price of four-hundred acres. he promised me 27c pr.

Mr Oakes as regards the negroes I Sent you to day I hope they will do tolerable well. I will Send you the Right & title assigned to Mr John A. Garrett from the former purchaser Showing planely the negro Girl nancy belonges to him a lone. I have not paid for the Girl yet. I have postponed the Settlement until I here from you. if it is Satisfactory to you, I will pay for her nothing less than $700 can buy her. please write me by Return mail Mr Garrett is waiting on me for an answer. if She will not do I will Give Mr Garrett an order for the Girl & please charge me for her Board up to the time he calls.

I have Given a Great history of matters more perhaps than is necessary Excuse me for Such long Epistles. please Give my Respects to all the famly. also Send my love to Susan.

A. J. McElveen to Z. B. Oakes,
Sumterville, S.C., 18 May 1854. (15)

yours came duly to hand this Evening.   I am under the impression they are nothing against young Garrett.   I Saw a certificate from our clerk here Stating they was no mortgage against him in the office.   I have Given him an order on you for the Girl.   The only dificulty about the case was this, his fathers creditors tryed to have the Girl Sold.   the young man wished to Get clear of her on that account.   he is off age, and he appears to be perfictly honest a bout it.

I leave here in the morning to See Dr McRae of Effingham Darlington S.C.   I cannot Get back here before tomorrow week.   please let me here from you by that time.   Iv bin carring the Surveyers chain all day.

A. J. McElveen to Z. B. Oakes,
Sumterville, S.C., 27 May 1854. (12)

nothing of intrust to write.   I would like to here from you.   Henry is Still on hand.   I have bin offred $1000 in two payments very Good paper but that dont Suite me. I will call on the man next week, & See if I cant strike a trade.   do let me here from you on Receipt of this.   I will leave here a Gain monday after the mail arrives.   do let me Know if Garrett has called for his Girl.   I hope McRae has Give you Some infermation a bout Joe.   I will be at Darlington C.H. the last of next week.   I will try & be down the middle of nex month to Stay a while   my Respects to all

P.S.   Mr J. S. Richardson called on me this Evening Saying he must Raise three hundred Dollars and offres me 20 pr cent, that is at the Rates anually to be paid next winter with Good Surity   he intends Seling negros to meet the pay-

ment   I can draw the note also as an advance on a certain
lot of negros he discribed to you   would Such arrangements
Suite you   I would like to accommodate him

A. J. McElveen to Z. B. Oakes,
Kingstree, S.C., 29 May 1854. (14)

on my arrival here I concluded to drop you a line.   nothing of importance to write.   I had the pleasure of the Doct
company in my Rout   he Says he will Get ceartificates
Statings facts in relation to Joe.   Dr Bass[47] of marion Knows
the fellow, and will Give a certificate as regards his Soundness,
when Mcrae Sold him   two other Doctors also.   Mcrae
Says he will attend to it and will write you this week also.
he Says it is very Strange the boy has bin Kept So long on
hand worthless & nothing has bin Said until Know.   I hope
Mcrae will furnish Such facts, that will lay the matter a Side
I will be in Sumterville thursday   I am offred 2 little negros
here for $900.   twins   they are nine or ten years old.
are they worth $800   I have offred Eight for them.

A. J. McElveen to Z. B. Oakes,
Sumterville, S.C., 30 May 1854. (4)

I am very Sory I could not here from you this Evening.
business is pretty brisk but prices are high yet.   I was offred a fellow to day for 950.   20.   weighs 180.   bad
teeth, two or three out in front.   I think I can buy him for
9.   do let me here from you on those points.   as regards
Richardson, I would like to do him a favour.   I refuse
letting any money out but in this case, I think it would turn

---

47. Probably Thomas Bass, physician, Marion District. U.S. Census, 1850,
    S.C., Marion, 31.

out to our advantage.   Mr Oakes how do the Girl Get on.   Garrette has just left me & will waite until monday for the money.   he contends for $700.   I told him if it was agreeable to your wish I would pay him on monday.   I did not Know until yesterday She was in the office Still.   do let me here from you   I leave in the morning and will be here a gain on Sunday.   monday is Sale day here & I think they will be two or three negros Sold

Goodealof Sickness here   I here the Small pox is prevaling in the city.

A. J. McElveen to Z. B. Oakes,
Sumterville, S.C., 5 June 1854. (1)[48]

You will please deliver to Mr John A Garrett or order the Girl nancy & oblige your &c.   charge me with board of the Girl up to 7th inst from time of her arrival in town.

P.S. I would be Glad if you would assist Mr Garrett in Selling the Girl   he is poore man and I believe him to be an honest man and any thing you can do will be highly appreciated by me

A. J. McElveen to Z. B. Oakes,
Sumterville, S.C., [6?] June 1854.[49] *(8)*

yours was duly Rec'   I have failed as yet to Sell henry they are one chance more for me.   I will attend to it this

---

48. This is the first of the Z. B. Oakes Papers as categorized by the order they were received rather than by chronology (see Calendar and Index, Oakes Papers). The mailing address on the back of the letter is "Mr Z B Oakes/Charleston/S C/No 7 State Street." Written in pencil next to A. J. McElveen's signature is "2v./F J Garrison/(36.139)/Nov. 11, 1891."   Francis Jackson Garrison was a son of William Lloyd Garrison.

49. Date of letter in Calendar and Index, Oakes Papers, is "4 June 1854." I read the date as 6 June 1854.

week.   I will be down next week if nothing happens to prevent.   I dont See any chance to buy up here attall.   I
want to Go to Richmond & buy Scrubs   I think more can
be made on Such than prime negros.   I Expect Mr Garrett
will call on you for his Girl.   I would like you to buy her
if posible as I can Get a young fellow for her if She has luck
in her burth.   that is to Risk   let me here from you on
receipt of this: as I could not buy the Girl from Mr Garrett,
I was honer bound to charge him no board   therefore you
will please charge me with the board up to 7 inst.

A. J. McElveen to Z. B. Oakes,
Sumterville, S.C., 7 [June?] 1854.[50](388)

yours came Safe to hand.   business is brisk but no
money in hand.   the boy Calep I bought of Mr H Bethune[51]
of Clerendon Sumter Dist I am Sory he is Runaway   I dont
think he will be out long if he comes up.   however I have
wrote to bethune begging him to taken as Soon as posible.
if you wish to write to Mr Bethune Direct your letters to Clear-
indon S.C.   I am offred 8 negros at the cost price.   I will
Give you a list and beg you to let me Know what they are
worth in market — one fellow — & wife and famly.

		Ages
Billy	very prime for his age	50
Rachael	his wife prime " "	40

---

50. Date of letter in Calendar and Index, Oakes Papers, is "7 Jan. 1854."
     I read the date as 7 June 1854. Most likely 7 June 1854 is the correct
     date because William T. Whaley, Jr., bought Caleb from Z. B. Oakes
     in March 1854 and wrote to Oakes in early June that Caleb had run
     away. He asked Oakes to help him find Caleb. See W. T. Whaley, Jr.,
     to Z. B. Oakes, 5 June 1854, Oakes Papers.
51. Probably Henry D. Bethune, planter, Sumter District. Teel, *1850 Cen-*
     sus, Sumter-District, dw. 162.

Jack 22 very prime Ben 20 prime
winny 17 pretty fare Girl. willis 14 prime
[Bow?] boy. delia, 7 alfred 3 the child is not yet
Recoverd from mesles all the Rest is well and Sound as far
as I Examined please let me have an answer by the last of
the week. the cost of the negros at Public out cry was
$4700 — forty Seven hundred Dollars. I dont think they
are more than $4000, at this price but that will not buy them.
do let me [hav?] Ideas and oblige your &c my Respects to
all

A. J. McElveen to Z. B. Oakes,
Sumterville, S.C., 6 July 1854. (395)

 I Saw Mr Blackwell.[52] he told me he was willing to do
what was Right & honerable in the boys case. he wants
you to Send the boy up. I wished him to Say how he was
willing to Settle the matter. he Said he could not Say until
he Saw him. Mr B. Says the Boy had soar legs once but
he thought they was intirely well, and had no Idia of any here
after a bout it. he Says Dr McColey looked at his legs
once but he cueard them himself. I wish you to have a
voice in this matter you will please write me how you
think best to Settle this matter if Mr B will Submit to
proper Reduction it is as well to Keep him, but I want you to
give me advise in the case how you would act. I believe
the Boy is worth more here than in the city that is nothing I must have my money back in Some way it must
be left in the Boy if I Keep him. I would like Mr Oakes
for you to call in too or three men and have the boy Estimated
what he is Really worth at this tim, and Send it to me it

---

52. Probably a Sumter District planter. Teel, *1850 Census, Sumter-District,*
  dws. 149, 431.

might have Some tendency to Settle the matter more Satisfactory   we have appointed to meet here on the 17 inst to
Settle the matter   therefore you will please Send the boy
up the 15th or 16th   our business is Such we cant meet here
before that time.   I leave here this afternoon and cannot
Get back a Gain Sooner than 15 or 16th   you will please
Give the boy a pass to Sumterville   he will be attended to.

Mr Oakes please tell Mrs oakes to tell Susan I hope She is
not fagot me & tell her I think more a bout her Since She
has bin absent than I Ever did   tell Susan to Send me her
Degarotype.   I think Susan might condecend to Send her
Respects to me Some times.   please tell Mrs oakes I hope
her & Miss lizz[53] will have a pleasant trip out.   my Respects to all.   {Mrs oakes will please hand Susan the little
note and oblige me, if they are no impropriety in my Sending it}

P.S. you will please call in Some physician & have Sam
thurough Examined & Send me his certifficate   I think it
will have some weight

A. J. McElveen to Z. B. Oakes,
Sumterville, S.C., 17 July 1854. (381)

we have Settled the matter in regard to boy Sam   Mr
blackwell taken him back & Give up my papers   also Give
me his note for $450 Mr Singletons & Davis note for $125, the
ballance I was due him which was $325.   he Gives me
Good Security on his note payable November   he Says
that is the best he could do as it is hard matter to Get money
at this time.   he will be compeled to Sell other negros.
he offres me a woman & too children for $1250.   the woman
30   too boys one 9 the other 2.   the woman will be con-
fined next winter.   I thought best to let the boy Go, as they

---

53. Miss lizz might be Z. B. Oakes's eldest daughter, C. E[lizabeth?]. U.S.
    Census, 1850, S.C., Charleston, 220.

would be Resk in Keeping him and Great deal trouble in Geting him well   we Settled without any dificulty.   I made the propersition first & he a Greed to it.   we boath lost   he lost the labour & I lost the intrust on four hundred & fifty Dollars for five months.   Therefore I hope the Settlement is Satisfactory to you hoping you will Satisfy Mr Dissaussure.   I Sold Henry to day for $950, with intrust fromdate.   the money cant be had at present.   note & good Security payable between this & next Jan.   young Ron Got a friend to buy him for him.   I can use all the above notes as cash if I wish in perchasing   they are a chance for me to Sell Doss too   Mr Mcfaddins are wanting him   one of them bought a Girl from me last fall   they will let me Know next month   I told them they could have Doss for $1500.   I was interduced to a Gentleman from mobile Dr Flemming   he tells me he wishes to purchase 30 negros next fall   20 men & 10 woman   he has bought negros in charleston.   he promised to meet me here in oct next and we will Go to charleston if I cannot Supply him here   I hope the prices will be Settled by the first of oct   Dr Flemming is a man of 60 years of age & appears to be a perfect Gentleman

Mr Oakes

I am Sory I let Mr allen have money   if I had Knew you was Short of funds I ceartainly would make him waite until the note was due   I will try & be wider a wake here after {what is a boy worth   likely   weighs 100 lbs.   without a blemish or defect}

A. J. McElveen to Z. B. Oakes,
Sumterville, S.C., 25 July 1854. (377)

yours came duly to hand this afternoon.   I am very Sory indeed things have turned out as they have but this case is one amongest a hundred.   I am at a lost to Know what to do.   I am Satisfied Dr Mcrae will do nothing from the fact that the time has bin to long, Since the boy was Sold however I will Right to him and State the particulars, and I would be Glad if you would write him also   I will See him the first of next month   I am Surprised he has not Sent on the certificates of too Doctors as he promised to do.   Mr Oakes you Know the Best way to persue in this case but I dont think we may depend on Dr Mcrae without a loaw Suite.   I am Sure I dont want you to loose any thing on my account and I hate very much to loose any thing my self   therefore tell McKay to Sue me here in Sumterville and let [us?] test the case for all parties can have a chance for a fare trial   I dont wish to take the advantage, but charleston will be too far for all parties to attend to court.   let me here from you what McKay intends doing.   I will do the best I can in buying. I think the boy is taken off to be Sold Since I wrote you   I will See in a day or too.   let you Know.   nothing new. fine crops in our country   let me here from the famley

A. J. McElveen to Z. B. Oakes,
Sumterville, S.C., 10 August 1854. (372)

I haste to drop you a line   I am anxious to here the State of the market.   I am called on to buy and at a lost to Know what to Give   in the first place I am offred too boys   one 13, weight 100 lbs   the other 16 weight 120 lbs.   the 16 years old boy must be Sent out the State   he has also a sore on one leg not very bad.   I can buy them boath for $1350   they are likely.   the dificulty is I cant Get my notes off for them.   I am called on to See Several others I cant well discribe.   do let me Know how they Sell that is different Kinds, and are they any Sale for them yet I beg my friends to hold on till next month.   I leave here in the morning and cant be here before the 22, as I have to Go Some 60 miles down the country to look at Some negros that I am perticularly called on to See.   I am also compeled to be at Darlington C.H. before I can be here.   as you will Receive this tomorrow, you will please drop me a note to Darlington C House.   the country is tolerable healthy at present.   Crops is very Good in this Section.   we have Great deal of Rain and prety heavy Storms   do let me here the Result of the Boy Joe.   if I can buy I will be down the first of next month.   I will try very hard to Get my notes off for Some Stock.   do let me here from all the famly

A. J. McElveen to Z. B. Oakes,

Kingstree, S.C., 14 August 1854. (367)

This will inform you Im in this Section and cannot do any thing as yet.   negros are held at the former prices. fellows has bin offred me too hundred Dollars higher than I could Sell them for in charleston.   you will please let me here from you on Recept of this note, and oblige me   please drop me a line to Darlington C.H. and Give me an Idea of the prices of negros.   I will See a lot of negros on my way to the court house.   I can make it Suite to call and See them on my Return   by hering from you I can no what to pay for them.   also I would be Glad to Know what I could Give with Safety for the two boys I discribed in my letter from Sumterville   too boys   one 13, the other 16.   boath likely   one must leave the State   has a little Soare on the leg, not very bad.   also please Give me all the informa-tion necessary.   one fellow offred me near no. 1 for $900. 5 feet 10 in.   20 years old.

A. J. McElveen to Z. B. Oakes,
Sumterville, S.C., 23 August 1854. (364)

yours came duly to hand last week   In my travels through the country, I find no chance to buy at prices   to Save cost therefore I must lay over until they are better in charleston   the fact is I cant buy negros up here at the prices you Gave me.   if I do it will be chance.   I Suppose they are no call for the Stock yet.   are they no traders in this Season ceartanly they must all be broke, or Give up business.   you will please write me on Recept of this.   I dont Know where to hunt Stock.   let me here from the famly   I am Sory to here you have bin Sick   I Keep very harty thank God.   I hope this will meet you all well.   5 negros will be Sold in a bout too weekes.   an Estate.   one woman & child   age 40, child 8 or 9.   prime fellow 35   prime do. 19 or 20.   boy 12. I want to buy them   what can I Stand on too or three years Credit that is, the prices and cash prices also.   do tell me what has become of Boy Joe.   whiteside wrote me he thought of being down next month.

A. J. McElveen to Z. B. Oakes,
Sumterville, S.C., 30 August 1854. (360)

yours was duly Red' this morning.   I am Glad to hear from the famly.   Great hopes you all will be blessed with health   I am Sorry the fever is prevaling in the city a Gain.[54]

---

54. Yellow fever, carried by steamers from Cuba, Florida, and elsewhere, reached Charleston by the last week of August 1854. It had also hit Savannah. In Charleston 203 persons died of it between September 3rd and the 16th. The mayor and city council proclaimed Friday, 22 September, "a day of Humiliation and Prayer." Concurrently, Jacksonville, Florida, quarantined "all vessels from Savannah or Charleston." The epidemic ended in Charleston in early November. Charleston *Daily Courier*, 22, 23, 29, 30 August, 5, 12, 19, 21, 29 September, 2 November 1854.

I am fearful these judgements are Sent on the place for the wicked Evils of the people.   however I will drop that we are wicked in the country.   I have bought the 2 Boys for $1300.   Mr Oakes I think they are a fine profit [ ]⁵⁵ them provided I have luck for I [do?] not Know where I could Get 2 aslikely [ ] a Gain for the money.   I Get them [ ] 30 days.   that will be the first of [ ]   I dont think it is worth while to Send them down before that time   they are on no Expence up to the time I pay for them   I think the largest boy will bring $800 at least, the other will bring $750 if they are any demand for Such Stock.   I hope to buy Some next week   one prime fellow in Jail for Sail now.   do write me what is the best price I can be Safe in Giving for prime fellows.   a man came through here the other [ ] and said he could not buy fellow[s?] [in?] charleston for less than 900. I hope [I?] will See him as he Expects to come [by?] [?] [R?] here   if I can Sell I will do So   I hope I will be able to Get of my notes next week.   the Exutor of the Est of Ma-Kensie⁵⁶ has power to Sell privately or publicly the 5 negros I discribed to you.   I will See him next week and if I can buy them I will do So.   too fellows likely   one 35   the other 20   a woman 40   boy 9.   a boy 12.   if I can buy, Mr Oakes I will Keep them all until oct.   you will please call on Mr W. H. Swinton⁵⁷ at Vandross St. and See a yellow boy who belongs to Mr Charles Delorme⁵⁸ of Sumter-

55. The brackets in this letter indicate sections that were faded or torn.
56. There were several planters in Sumter District surnamed McKenzee or McKenzie. Teel, *1850 Census, Sumter-District*, dws. 1513, 981, 1551, 1553, 1557.
57. Probably William H. Swinton, Charleston lumber merchant. Charleston city directory (1855), 103.
58. Charles H. Delorme, a planter, co-published the Sumter *Dispatch* in 1858. Teel, *1850 Census, Sumter-District*, dw. 1883; Nicholes, *Historical Sketches*, 1: 97.

ville and Say what you are willing to Give for him.   Mr
Delorme called on me this morning and beg me to call your
attention to the Boy.   Mr D. Son lives with Mr Swinton.
if you can buy him I can Settle with Mr Delorme here and
have the title properly Executed hear also

A. J. McElveen to Z. B. Oakes,
Sumterville, S.C., 1 September 1854. (324)

yours is Just at hand.   I made no calculation to Send
the boys down Sooner than three weekes   I intended to
buy more and Send them all together.   however I will try
and Send them on Tuesday if you are ceartin of Selling them
I think they would be better off up here to Remain on hand
as they are no Expence and very little work to do.   I want
to buy a fellow on monday if I can.   they are one in Jail
for Sail and prehaps more will be Sold by the Sheriff   I
understood the Sheriff has nothing to do with the fellow in
Jail and his master will be here on monday.   dont Send to
R.R before Tuesday.   Susan Sends her love to you and all
Enquiring friends.   I am very much oblige to you for fowerd-
ing the letter.   they was in Boston on the 25th Aug.   She
was injoying herself very much.   I Suppose they was all
well   nothing particularly mentioned in regard to health
please Send my Respects to them   please Say to [haurel-
ton?] norton his uncle Says he must come up if the fever Gets
any worse   I was very Sick last night and thought the fevar
was coming on but I feel better to day.   {Stamps is Just
out.}

A. J. McElveen to Z. B. Oakes,
Sumterville, S.C., 9 September 1854. (356)

yours came Safe to hand   it has bin out of my power to
buy any thing this weeke.   I leave here Tuesday first for a

rout down the country   I hope I will be able to Send you Some Stock by the time I Return   I would be Glad if you would Write me by mondays mail how the fever is and the State of the market, and how all the famly is   I will be absent for some ten days.   I met Bob Cook[59] here the other day.   he is in private conveyance and watingman.   he Says he wants to pick up Some old negroes.   he is on his way up the country.   Mr Disher[60] came in yesterday, will be here a day or too.

P.S. I have Just bin informed you have had a tremendous Gail in the city.[61]   I am very Sory for it.   I Suppose they are Great damage from it.   I have Just met with Mr Barr[62] from allabama   he is on his way to Richmond.   he tells me prime negro fellows are worth $1050   also he tells me Mr Lumkin[63] wrote him fellows in Richmond is worth ten fifty.   do let me Know if E. H. Jones are dead   it is Reported he died with the yellow fever in the city   he went

59. Robert Cook, probably a fellow slave trader. Tadman, *Speculators and Slaves*, 35–36, 272.

60. Possibly Robert W. Disher, planter and slave trader, Charleston Neck, Charleston District. Tadman, *Speculators and Slaves*, 35–36, 272; Charleston city directory (1855), 30; U.S. Census, 1860, S.C., Charleston, 168.

61. Thursday morning, 7 September 1854, "a Violent Storm" hit Charleston. It was "one of the severest and most destructive . . . felt . . . for many years." Hardest hit were the wharves along East Bay and the merchandise stored on them. Estimates of the damages on the wharves exceeded a quarter million dollars. Charleston *Daily Courier*, 8 September, 9 September 1854.

62. Probably James A. Barr, an Alabama slave trader. Tadman, *Speculators and Slaves*, 36, 272; J. A. Barr to Dear Sir, 11 September 1854, A. J. McElveen to Z. B. Oakes, 23 September 1854, Oakes Papers.

63. Robert Lumpkin, prosperous Richmond slave trader. Richmond city directories (1852, 1860), as cited in Manuscripts, Box 11, Negro and Slavery—Notes, etc., pp. A95, A97AA, Frederic Bancroft Papers; Bancroft, *Slave-Trading in the Old South*, 101, 102–103.

down the other day   Mr Oakes capt G. W. White called on
me the other day and wants you to buy him a Second hand
piano as I cannot Go down.   he has a fellow for Sail   also
he will Send his cotton down Soon as Ready   if you can
oblige him do so   Supposed from $150 to 200 would buy
pretty fare one   please let me Know by mondays mail.

A. J. McElveen to Z. B. Oakes,
Sumterville, S.C., 11 September 1854. (351)

you will See from the inclosed letters they are false Repre-
sentations Sent in to induce you to do what is not right.   Dr
witherspoon did not Give Dr Gelzer[64] any Such infermation
as he asserted   therefore you will please See into the Matter
and heave a fare test.   I would call on the Doct for withe-
spoons letter.   I will Send his back.   also I think I left
Sollomons Reciept with you   Mr Solomons Says he is Ready
to prove the woman Sound when I bought her   therefore
I am at my Rows End.   I hope you will not allow men to
deceive you Mr Oakes   they are very few men you can rely
on.   I leave here tomorrow to attend a Sale   wont be
back in ten days, or too weeks   this is all I can do in this
case   I hope you will Settle it with out any loss on our
part.   please write me by the 22nd the result of this case.

A. J. McElveen to Z. B. Oakes,
Kingstree, S.C., 18 September 1854. (347)

this will inform you I am in the low country and cannot
be in Sumterville before the 24 or 25   I bought one boy and

---

64. Thomas L. Gelzer, Summerville physician. T. L. Gelzer to Z. B. Oakes,
    6 December 1853, 12 April, 26 April, 8 September 1854, n.d. (Ms. Am.
    322/141), Oakes Papers.

Sent him to Sumterville last week.   I will try and Send him down this day week   if posible, the 25.   I cant Get up to Sumter well before the time a bove Stated.   I have Several calls to make on the way, and I hope to buy before I Get home.   I paid for the boy in notes I had in hand.   he is likely   14 years old   weighs a little over one hundred. Good teeth   all right   Good title.   if they are any danger in Sending down do let me Know.   please let me Know how the fever is prevaling.   let me here from you on Recpt of this   I was offred 5 fellows.   I could not buy them   too Scrubs, three second class boys.   I offred for the 3 best $2400.   I thought that Enough   nothing less than nine could buy them   So you See it is a hard matter to buy at prices to make any thing.   I will Keep trying. do let me here from the famly.

A. J. McElveen to Z. B. Oakes,

Sumterville, S.C., 23 September 1854. (325)

I have Just arrived here and no news from you.   I am Sorry you have not wrote me in answer of mine from Kingstree.   I also met manser this Evening from Richmond   he Says they are but little doing there.   I Receivd a letter from Mr Barr[65] which I will Enclose to you   I have only one Boy in my travels.   I Suppose I had better Sell him to manser if I can as the fever is So bad.   if I dont Sell him I will Keep him until you wish me to Send him down   do write me as Soon as you Get this, and Give me all the news of importance. if manser will Go with me perhaps he can buy as many fellows as he wants.   I here [Mr?] Martin[66] is in town.   tell him

---

65. Probably J. A. Barr to Dear Sir, 11 September 1854, Oakes Papers. Letter discusses prices in Richmond. Z. B. Oakes's name is not mentioned.

66. Possibly W. J. Martin of New Orleans, who corresponded with Oakes about the slave trade in Charleston. Letters from W. J. Martin, Oakes Papers.

I am Sorry I cant be with him.   do let me Know how you
all are & how you Get a long with the fever   let me here
from the famly at the north   I hope you will not Expose
your Self and Keep clear of the fever.   I am Sorry it is Rag-
ing to Such extent   do take cear of the children.   Give
them all my Respects.

A. J. McElveen to Z. B. Oakes,
Sumterville, S.C., 29 September 1854. (327)

this will inform you I am doing all I can in the way of
trading but it is very little   I have bin on a journey with
Mr mansur.   we have the promise of 3 fellows on monday
but I think it doubtful of his Getting them   he offred $900
for them and if they conclude to take it they will bring them
in on monday   he bought a Girl for 650.   Small Size
the man has promised to take my notes So I will Get the
money from mansur   he will call and pay you on his Return   he cant Get his checks cashed here   I want him to
take my boy.   the boy is likely   his weight is 102.   in
his 14th year   what is he worth in charleston.   he cost
me $710.   blanket & close & hat 7 dollars.   I thought
I would let mansur have him at 750 & pay you also on his
Return.   advise me what to do.   if the fellow comes I will
Get 20 dollars on the head.   please let me here from you
immediately.   he bought 50 year old man to day for $400.
{Whiteside is anxious to Know when you want him.}   {how
is the fever prevaling}

A. J. McElveen to Z. B. Oakes,
Sumterville, S.C., 4 October 1854. (338)

yours was duly Received   I think mansur is whipt
out   he is awfully disappointed   two negros Runaway.

one of them the Girl I was to pay for with my notes.   if She is not apprehended this week I will Get her as Soon as She is.   mansur dont want the boy.   he is too small. if martin is in town prehaps he will take him   mansur will try and Sell for me.   the fact is the boy will Sell if any negro will as Soon as a customer comes a long.   I hope the fever will Soon abate and business commence.   I am Glad to hear you all Keep well.   my health is very Good at present.   please Give my love to all the famly, in the city & at the north.   if I Should buy four or five negros I think I will take them to Lowerys Turnout, Barnwell Dist   prehaps my old customers may buy.   let me hear from you by mansur

P.S. I would be Glad if you would Get capt Whites pianno he wishes a second hand one not over $150.   if you can Get one worth buying do let me Know.   he wants it Sent up on the Steammer DeKalb to Murrys Ferry.[67]   do let me Know if you will Get it.

A. J. McElveen to Mr. Mcbride,[68]
Sumterville, S.C., 30 October 1854. (333)

I drop you a line in haste.   if this should meet you a live you will please inform me if Mr Oakes is in the city.   I have wrote to him two or three times and cannot hear from him   prehaps he is Sick.   do let me Know By return

---

67. The steamer *DeKalb* carried freight from Charleston to "Wright's Bluff, Murray's Ferry, and all the intermediate landings on the Santee River." Murray's Ferry, Williamsburg District, crossed the Santee River. Charleston *Daily Courier*, 22 September, 18 October, 15 December 1854; Boddie, *History of Williamsburg*, 61, 207–208, 324, 326.

68. M. McBride, Charleston broker and auctioneer, 14 State Street. Charleston city directory (1855), 67; Charleston *Daily Courier*, 26 January 1855.

mail what is the matter.   I want to make a purchase in a
few days and wrote him for advise.   how is prime negros
Selling   are they any demand for any Kind   will you
please let me Know what progress the fever is making.   I
Saw Wm Wright[69] from Savanah on his way from new york.
he told me he left his famly in new york.   he told me he
had Engaged 12 fellows to Mr Campbell[70] (if I dont mistake
the name) of Baltimore, at $1200 Round.   prehaps Wright
called on his return.   he Said he was Going through Agusta.
Mc let me hear from you immediately.   do let me hear
from the Miss Mitchells.   Give Mrs Kinsid my Respects your
Sister if you cant make out the name

A. J. McElveen to Z. B. Oakes,

Sumterville, S.C., 9 November 1854. (311)

    yours was Recd in due time.   they was nothing to write
worth while   the lot of negros I cant Buy.   they are too
high.   others are offred me   I have not Seen them   do
let me Know the State of the market   I think I will buy one
or too and Send them down by whitesides.   I will Send him
down next week.   I cant close the trade for Doss   Mcfaddin backed out from the first propusition and offred me a
prime fellow and $300 for him.   if you wish me to try him
a Gain Send him up on Saturday.   I asked Mcfaddin $400.
he wants to See him work.   I am to look at a Girl to day,
and a fellow to morrow   please Give my Respect to Mrs
Oakes and famly.

---

69. A Savannah slave trader who corresponded extensively with Z. B. Oakes.
    See Calendar and Index, Oakes Papers.
70. Probably B. M. or Walter L. Campbell, both Baltimore slave traders.
    Bancroft, *Slave-Trading in the Old South,* 316, 317 n. 8.

A. J. McElveen to Z. B. Oakes,
Sumterville, S.C., 11 November 1854. (310)

yours have just came to hand.   I would be Glad if you would Send Doss up monday, if you have not Sent him   he may be here   I just Got in.   I refused a boy at $650 35 or 40 years of age.   looks well for the age.   a bout the Size of adam.   I am to leave here to morrow to See three or four mostly women.   I cannot buy any thing like no 1. boys for less than $1000 here.   the Rail R. & Turpentine men[71] Gives $200 hire, and will pay $1000 when they can buy them.   a man from Ala. is here and wants a blacksmith, I was informed.   I Know the Gentleman and I Know he has the cash but I do not Know the fellow will Suite him but I am anxious to let him See him   there fore please have the boy Sent here by monday if this Reaches in time   Mr Patrick will leave as Soon as he Settles his fathers Estate   I think he will leave a bout Tuesday   Mr Mcfaddens fellows I think is near No 1.   he has too and will not take less than $1000.

A. J. McElveen to Z. B. Oakes,
Sumter District, S.C., 17 November 1854. (317)[72]

I Send you two negros by Mr Whiteside, namly Betsy & Sarah.   I hope you will do well with them.   I am Sorry they are not the Kind to Sell Readly.   however I think they will pay a profit.   it is not Easy to buy likely young negros, Especially Boys & fellows.   I have to day bought 5 negros

---

71. Sumter and Williamsburg Districts developed a significant business in turpentine, especially after the Civil War. Gregorie, *History of Sumter County*, 486; Boddie, *History of Williamsburg*, 536.
72. Back of letter indicates that McElveen sent it to Oakes by way of Whiteside.

for $1800.   three [Groom?][73] ones   two children   I
hope they will pay fine profit also.   I will Send them down
on monday.   I barganed for a likely Girl this morning at
$650   if nothing happens to prevent, I will Send her on mon-
day.   they are some dificulty in title, but I am disposed to
try it   I wish her Sent out the State as Early as convenant.
I am not to pay for her until She is Sent off   please write
me on Recept of this.   price Sarah & Betsy $1000.

my Respects to all the famly

A. J. McElveen to Z. B. Oakes,

Sumterville, S.C., 18 November 1854. (315)

yours of yesterday came duly to hand with the fellow
Doss   I will call on Mcfadden in a few days   I wish to
See Mr Mahoney before I Go to Mcfadden.   I have Seen
the boy you Speake of and offred Mr Mahoney $850 Some
time Since   I dont believe he is as Good a boy as adam.
I may be mistaken   I Saw him last Summer   perhaps he
has improved Since.   I dont think Mr Mahoney will take
less than nine for him.   I am doubtful I cant buy him
without   the market is better than has bin.   you See how
dificult it is to buy Saleable negros   however that is no
Reason I Should buy Such that will not Sell.   I am tired
of doing nothing.   if I cant do better I would be Glad to
have your advise.   do let me Know the hiest price I can
Give for Such boys as adam to live at it.   if I cant make
a trade with Mcfadden what will I do with Doss.

P S. please Send to R R. on monday   I will Send down
5 negros, and prehaps 6.   the likely Girl I Spoke of, I am
not ceartain of Getting.   if I send her please Ship her as
Soon as posible   I am ceartain no person will hunt her up.

---

73. [Groom?] is probably "Grown."

A. J. McElveen to Z. B. Oakes,
Sumter District, S.C., 19 November 1854. (318)[74]

I send you 5 negros By R R hoping they will please you though they are not the Kind I wish to buy.   it is very hard to buy Such as will Sell Readly but not withstanding this lot of negros ought to pay a profit if negros Sell attall   do let me hear from you on Receipt of this.   the Girl I could not buy without paying a part down and I concluded to not take her   I will Send you Mr Otys[75] letters Giving the State of the Richmond market.   Doss arrive Safely.   I am offred $6000 Bonds at ten pr cent discount payable in thousand Dollar instalments annually in four years if I dont make mistake. please Give Mrs O. and famly my Best Respects

A. J. McElveen to Z. B. Oakes,
Sumterville, S.C., 24 November 1854. (321)

yours of the 22d was duly Recd this afternoon.   I have just Returned from Seeing Mr Mahoney   he is not ready to Sell his boy yet, thinking negros will be higher.   I hope he will realise what he anticipates.   I will See what I can do with Doss next week.   I have him doing Some work to take as a Specimen with him.   I thought of Bying Mcfaddens two fellows and take them to Richmond.   a nother fellow in his neighbor hood is offred at the Same price $1000. he is no 1, no doubt.   I think it would pay to take them to Richmond if they are worth $1150 to 1200.   the parties wants me to take this Girl and Send her off.   they are no

---

74. Back of letter indicates that McElveen sent it to Oakes by way of "Servents on R.R."
75. Thomas Otey, Richmond slave trader. Letters from Thomas Otey, Oakes Papers.

dificulty   only the Guardian one of the children can Sine the title   it is old Enough   they have all come to the conclusion to have $700.   She is likely but a little too low. I think I might do well to take three or four to Richmond do let me Know what you think of the arrangement   I can buy the fellows on Short credit

As regards the negros I Sent down to you they are ceartanly cheap but will not Sell Readly.   that is all I hated a bout the purchase.   I would be Glad if you would See Dr [Simms?].   he has little Tolerable likely Girl   his brother Says he intends Selling this winter   I dined at his place to day with his famly   the Doctors wife told me She looked for him up the 2nd day of Decr.   that is Saturday week. if he will Sell her I will meet him on that day   She is worth a bout $600 to 650.   16.   if you wish to See me please drop me a line I will come at any time.   I may not come before Jan.

A. J. McElveen to Z. B. Oakes,
Mayesville, S.C., 29 November 1854. (322)

I have not bought any thing Since I wrote to you last. Some of the prime fellows I Expected to Get is in the woods yet.   I dont See any chance to buy Such as would Suite Richmond market   however they are one fellow offred me for one thousand Dollars.   5 feet 7 inches.   weighs 180 lbs   no Surplus flesh.   he is prime   I offrd $900   I dont think he can be bought for less than $1000.   as for Doss I cant make the Exchange.   McFaddins boy is not worth more than nine in market   consequently I did not trade   I offrd to take 400   he would not Give it.   I am offrd a woman and 3 children for $1400.   the woman 22   very likely   bad teeth but tall and likely   the Eldest child 6 or 7   likely Girl   the next Boy 3   likely

the third one year old.   the woman a first Rate Seamstress   make fine Shirts &c   cook also   I dont think
they are very high   do write me if the market can afford
the price   please let me Know by friday or Saturdays mail
I can have until the 15 of Decr. to pay for them.   I hope
you done the best that could be done for capt woods & my
Brother is Getting these boys Sold   Excuse this as I am on
my way to Sumterville.   I think I will be down by the 18
of Dec.   My Respects to all the famly

A. J. McElveen to Z. B. Oakes,
Sumterville, S.C., 1 December 1854. (306)

your two letters was duly Received and contents noticed.
I am very Sorry to hear the market is So dull.   I thought
at least the lot of negros I Sent namly 7, would pay five hundred Dollars.   I cant buy negros as low as them without
I meet men in Great Strain for money.   however I am
Satisfied you will do the best you can.   Mr Hariot Says he
will Give $1800 for the last lot I bought and pay my Expences
after them.   the lot of negros was bought in his neighbour-
hood.   as for Mr Kerby, they are Several young men of the
Sam name and without I new his christain nam I cannot tell
a bout the title.   I believe my Brother Knows them all as
well as I do   they all have negros I believe and they are all
my friends as far as I Know, and I hope you will do the best
you can for him   I Expect to buy the Girl Spoke of Some
time Since   the title is not very Good but I believe Eventually I will be Safe   you will please allow me to take her
on my own Resposability that is Giving my title and Run all
Risk   I Know the parties   I will Send her on Tuesday if
I take her   prehaps it might be longer.   I want to buy
the famly with the Seamstress.   they are not high and
any body will Buy Such qualified Servants   they cant

be bought for less than $1400.   likely woman with three chil-
dren   the oldest large enough to commence nursing.   the
second 3   the last one   please let me hear from you immediately as regards the Runaway   I informed the owner
of the Girl last Evening.   I will let the former owner Know
a bout Caleb   the man I purchased Caleb from is dead but
I Know his brother will do any thing he can for me in Geting
him apprehended.   you will please answer my letter from
maysville.

A. J. McElveen to Z. B. Oakes,
Sumterville, S.C., 4 December 1854. (303)

  I am Sory you did not answer my last letters.   I heard
from you by my Brother but I would bin Glad to heard by letter   Some 8 or 10 negros Sold to day tolerable low but not
the Kind to Sell   6 in family Sold for $1675.   do let me
Know what the famly is worth namly Good Seamstress and
three children.   perhaps I may Get a letter from you this
Evening   the mail comes in late   I Expected to Get a letter last Evening.   a Gentleman Spoke to me to day Saying a friend of his west wanted to purchase from 80 to 150
negros prime   is willing to Give market price if Such offred
please let me Know   will buy in famleys   please let me
hear from you, on Recipt of this
  my Respects to all the famly.

A. J. McElveen to Z. B. Oakes,
Sumterville, S.C., 5 December 1854. (302)

  will the market warrent $900 for prime negro man
weight 180 lbs.   5 f 7 in   a bout 25 years old.   I cannot Get him for less.   Mr Brunson Says I can have him to
Sell on Commissions by advancing 2 or 3 hundred Dollars as

---

he is in want of that amount.[76]   what do you think of the arrangement   please let me Know and I will be able to Send the fellow down by Saturday first.   I was not able to Give you this infermation yesterday as I wrote you.   I hope you will Excuse me   if I cant hear from you a bout the fellow I will advance on him and Send him on Saturday.   I Suppose the market is miserable about this time

A. J. McElveen to Z. B. Oakes,
Sumterville, S.C., 11 December 1854. (297)

I Send you Six negros I hope will please you   better than I Represented though I am Sory I bought them.   woman & three children $1400   Smart $825. Mr W. H. Brunsons Boy arthur, I advanced $200.   he wishes you to do the best you can. $900 clear will be Satisfactory Dr. Moses[77] was not disposed to accomodate me as I told you. however, I hope you willnot think hard.   Mr Solomons would Give me $1500 to day for the famly if he could Raised the money.   She is fine Seamstress, and will Suite any persons wishing Such a negro.   I hope you will Get a little advance on the negros   if not hold on as long as you can. I want to Go west this winter   Mr Brown[78] is hear and wants nothing but what is Strickley prime and Says he will be hear in January and is willing to Join me in a lot of negros. capt G. W. White is on his way to ala   is very Sory I could

---

76. Probably W. H. Brunson's slave, Arthur. The 1850 census, Sumter District, lists two planters named William H. Brunson. William Hartwell Brunson, from Middle Salem, was also a Methodist Episcopal clergyman. See A. J. McElveen to Z. B. Oakes, 11 December 1854, Oakes Papers; Teel, *1850 Census, Sumter-District*, dws. 238, 1430; Teel, *1860 Census, Sumter-District*, dw. 1475.
77. Perhaps Colonel Montgomery Moses.
78. Probably S. N. Brown.

not Go.   I Send Doss with him.   he Says he will do the best he can for me.   one of his acquaintance is wanting a Smith   I directed him to Sell him and not bring him back. I am Satisfied he will do the best he can   white is not willing to take any negros that will be any trouble in Geting a long he dont think hard a bout [Sining?] the note.   he will be Back by the 8th of Jan, if nothing happens to prevent him I hope my arrangements willnot displease you.   I have clothed Smart   Mr Brunson wishes you to put a Suite on his boy.   Mr oakes the two boys might Give you the Slip. dont let them have any liberty going out.   please Give the negros clothes I Send them that need them   if you Sell Smart do have him Sent out the State if posible.   please let me hear from you on Recipt of this

A. J. McElveen to Z. B. Oakes,
Sumterville, S.C., 20 December 1854. (286)

yours came duly to hand   I have nothing to Say further.   I new the negros would not Suite the market.   I hope you will not Sell them under cost.   when I agreed to take them I did not think of Selling them in charleston.   I think Charleston one of the porest markets for any thing.   if you can affard to Keep the negros on hand a while, I will come and take them off if you have no objection.   please let me hear from you on Receipt of this   they are two negros offred me.   I am at a lost to make an offer, but I dont intend to offer until I hear what price is put on them   young fellow 20   Girl 17.   boath likely   if I find them likely what are they worth cash   I have a greed to take a Girl at Jan Good Size nurse at $500.   do let me Know if they are futher decline in prices.   they will be Some Sold hear on a credit the first day of Jan.   tolerable prime fellows   one Blacksmith.

---

you will please Give my Respects to all the famly.   may you all have merry chritsmast.

A. J. McElveen to Z. B. Oakes,
Sumterville, S.C., 23 December 1854. (283)

your two letters came Safely to hand.   I cannot posebly leave before the first of Jan.   I hope trade will be better a bout that time   nothing is done about christmast, any where.   I am buying Some negros to take out if they are no posible chance to make any thing on them in town   I bought 2 boys to day a bout 11 & 12   weights one 80 lbs, the other 82.   likely full fare chaps.   I am to pay $1000 for them the first day of Jan.   I am ceartain all is Right, without Some unknown occurrence   I have the bargained witnessed.   I Expect to buy more next week & Several is to be Sold here on the first day of Jan.   Some a part cash and Some all credit.   you will please make Some arrangements with the Bank   moses Tells me the bank orders no discounting at the present.   therefore if I cant Get money here please Permit me a draft.   I cant tell how much I will need.   the 2 Boys 500 Each   the Girl I have ingaged at 500.   I think I will buy 3 fellows Sold by the commissioner one third cash   pretty prime fellows   I Know all abot them   they are too more I discribed to you   young fellow and Girl 20 & 17 years.   I will See them also next week and I think they are a chance to buy them.   Maj. Green of Bishopville wrote me he has too or three for Sale   one fellow in the woods I am prety ceartai of Geting   I think he is over 6 feet, a bout 20 age   I have put out word I have bought him   I think he will come to me.   Green wants $1000 for hm.   what is the hiest for Such a fellow   he is Extra, no mistake.   the boy is a fine waggoner   Extraordanary hosler.   Green would not take 1500 for him if he would Stay with him but he has Spoilt him by bad management. the Girl bad title I told you about if I Go a way I will buy her I believe all the negros I can Git on time I will take at the right prices and making [arrange?][79] I will Give orders on you at 60 days [or so?] if that will Suite please let me hear from you on Recipt of this. I wish you all merry christmast & happy new year please send my Respects to Susan & tell her I wish her merry christmast & happy new year Say to her for me if you please I want to hear from her very much.

A. J. McElveen to Z. B. Oakes,
Sumterville, S.C., 29 December 1854. (280)

I have just Received yours this Evening I am very Sorry I was absent consequently I could not come in time to leave for abbeville. I hope they are no time lost in making Sails. I have bought 5 negros all Single. I hope they will pay, but what will I do with no money. can you posebly Send whitesides up Sunday or monday, to take the negros down. do try and Get a note from the president of the bank to Moses to let me have money. I cant Get the negros without money Moses Says he has money, but no orders to discount I cant See what policy they have in doing business this way as the draffs are paid promply. I will Get all the indulgence I can in the payment of the negros. I think Some of them will let me of by paying half cash & thirty days for the ballence. I look for Capt White from Ala. on the 6th I wish to See him before I leave here.

my Respects to all the famly.

---

79. [arrange?] is probably "arrangements." Page is torn.

A. J. McElveen to Z. B. Oakes,
Sumterville, S.C., 31 December 1854. (276)

yours came duly to hand this Evening.   I just Seen Moses   he Says the instructions was to let out no more money until further orders.   he Says what can he do further   as agent he is bound to obey orders.   he is wating for orders from the banks   I hope it will be arranged Soon. if posible I will Send the negros or bring them.   I think I had better come.   if I can Get the negros without the money look for me or the negros and prehaps boath on Tuesday. you will please call on the capt. of the steamerboat Florida.[80] I have just ascertained he wants 6 fellows.   I Saw a Friend from florida who Says negros is very high.   fellows are bringing $1000 and over if prime.   I can rely on the infermation as I have bin acquainted with him all my life   he lives in Florida.   I will See witherspoon tomorrow I hope and ascertain if the fellow can be bought.   I think it doubtful [ ][81] as the fellow is a carpenter.   I am fearful this will not Reach in time as they are difrent arrangements with the mail

PS. one negro just come for me Since I [commenced?] writing & I hear one has runaway   they be [Some?] 20 Sold   I hear of 5 on the way.

A. J. McElveen to Z. B. Oakes,
Sumterville, S.C., 6 January 1855. (272)

I Send you two boys   they are boath all right, that is clear of whipping   a little scar on the fore head of

---

80. With R. H. Stewart [Stuart?] as master, the steamer *Florida* provided service to Florida, especially points on the St. John's River, including Jacksonville, Picolata, Pilatka, and Black Creek. Charleston *Daily Courier*, 14 October, 1 November 1854.
81. Page is torn.

William   you can recommend them as Good ordely boys. I think nearly as likely as any I Ever bought.   I complied as Soon as I arrived yesterday.   My brother was wating for me from the day before.   Cost   William $780 harvey $600.   papers 7.50 cts   Jail fees 5.00.   I wish you to let me Know if you want me to take off the negros by the 15th.   I will be absent nearly all next week.   I think I will be here by the 13th or 14th.   any how, white came in with me yesterday.   Doss was not Sold when he left, but Says he will be well taken cear off, and Says no doubt he will be Sold Soon.   it is hard for him to tell whether I can do well with a lot of negros   he Says times is pretty hard. however I am ready and willing to do as you think best.   do let me hear from you Soon

A. J. McElveen to Z. B. Oakes,
Sumterville, S.C., 13 January 1855. (270)

Yours has just come to hand.   I am holding off at present.   howevery I hope times will be better Soon.   I think as I told you Florida is the best market yet, but I dont think any market is very much at this time.   I have just Received a note from Miss Fleming, the lady I bought George & lefegett from — Statius   She will take boath the boys back as I could not Settle with them by Returning one   I think I had best return boath.   you will please Send lefegett up monday if posible or Tuesday Will do, as I want to come down on wednesday, and I wish to Settle the matter before I leave   do Send Jack with him as it will be hard for the boy to Get up without help   if any one could put him on the wilmington & manchester Road I can meet him at the depot.   please let me hear from you immediately.   I have just heard from Doss   he was not Sold on the 7th inst.

P.S. Mr John K. white, hamburg Ala., he Says he dont think it best to be hasty in Selling   by taking some time he

Can do better and will do the best he Can.   he Says they are a Good many negros in market, marion alaba.   I have Every Confidence in white as a man of Jenuine principle. if you thin[k?] best to write and Give him your [no?][82] as regards Selling &c I will answer his and Direct him to write you.

A. J. McElveen to Z. B. Oakes,
Sumterville, S.C., 16 January 1855. (259)

Will you advise me the course to persue in this Case Miss Fleming is not willing to take one boy without the other therefore I am at a lost to Settle the matter as She has my note and will not Give it up.   I Give my note before I took the boys to charleston   we are to Settle the matter on Friday if posible   do let me here from you by that time   I wrote you on last Saturday and thought I would hear to day.   the 19 inst is the day we are to Settle   do you wish me to take the negros off.   I have no notion to buy here.   too boys Sold to day.   one $1150   the other $1100.   boath inferior to Benbows[83] Jacob.   on two years Credit.   Estate Sale   Mr J. B. Brogdon[84] is begging me to advance $600 on his negros.   I tell him that is left to you.   he Says he must have Six hundred Dollars by the first monday in Febuary or he will be compeled to let the Sherieff Sell.   Mr Brunson is teasing me to have Something down with his boy arthur do let me here from you in haste

---

82. [no?] is probably "note." Last letters are faded.
83. Probably H. L. Benbow. See H. L. Benbow to Z. B. Oakes, 4 March 1855, Oakes Papers.
84. Planter who helped in the construction of the Clarendon District courthouse and jail at Manning. He is not to be confused with John Bagnal Brogdon. See A. J. McElveen to Z. B. Oakes, 20 August 1853, Oakes Papers, and note 9 above; Teel, *1850 Census, Sumter-District*, dw. 440; Nicholes, *Historical Sketches*, 1: 111, 518.

A. J. McElveen to Z. B. Oakes,
Sumterville, S.C., 16 January 1855. (260)

I drop you a note through capt hammet[85] hoping it will reach in time.   I am at a lost to Know what course to per-sue   Miss Fleming is not willing to take one of the boys without the other, George & lefeget   they have my note which I have before I taken the boys to charleston   I am anxious to hear from you by Friday the 19th inst, the day which we are to meet and Settle the Matter   will you please let me hear from you without delay   I wrote you last Satur-day.   Mr Brogdon is wanting me to advance on his negros $600.   he is compeled to have money first monday in Feb or the Sheriff will Sell property.   Mr Brunson is teasing me a bout his boy arthur.   can I do any thing for them here I want to come down on Saturday the 20th inst.   do you wish me to take the negros off   too boys Sold to day for $115 & 1100.   I have but little notion of buying at any price.

Bulgre & De Vane[86] to A. J. McElveen,
Montgomery, Ala., 19 January 1855. (263)[87]

Sir yours of 18 inst just recd in answer.   business in our line exceedingly dull.   very few sales are made at any price for cash owing to the scarcity of mony & low stage of

---

85. Possibly Jared B. N. Hammet, Sumterville lawyer and clerk of council (1848). Teel, *1850 Census, Sumter-District*, dw. 1891; Sumter (Sumter-ville) *Banner*, 5 April 1848, 7 August 1850.

86. O. L. Bulger and P. R. DeVane, Montgomery slave trading firm. Tad-man, *Speculators and Slaves*, 265.

87. Back of letter is addressed to Col. A. J. McElveen, Charleston, S.C., care of Z. B. Oakes, Esq. The salutation is "A. J McElveen Esq/Charles-ton SC."

our rivrs; for as yet we have had no rain but few fellows in market & they are held at from $1,000 to $1200.   Asto the [proble?] worth of your seamstress & 3 children we cant say. Your seamstress & 1 child if a good hand to cut & fit & likely would sell for 1300 to 1500   the child would not add any thing to her price.   boys 14 to 15 years old would Sell for $900 to $1,000 if likely   if you visit our city we would be pleased to have you call on us   we will do the best we can for you   we hope times will be better but at present they are very dull & we have no encouragement to offer.

J. K. White to Z. B. Oakes and A. J. McElveen,
23 January 1855. (268)

The letter from Mr McElveen came some few days since Contents noticed.   I am very sorry to say that the boy Doss is still on my hands and not sold yet and you both may think that I do not persevere enough but my dear Sirs that is not it   You say times are hard with you but I just never heard such complaint about [mona?]; Cotton is down which you Know is our only chance and the rivers are down so if cotton was worth any thing we could not get it into market; but I [mark?] you to be patient as I will effect a sale as soon as pissible and you shall hear from me immediately afterwards You both Know it requires a man of a deal of patience to trade in negro property   nothing more but yours truly

A. J. McElveen to Z. B. Oakes,
Sumterville, S.C., 3 February 1855. (266)

I arrived here Safe on Thursday Evening.   the night train broke down a bout Eleven o clock the Evening I left consequentely I was detaind until the morning train came up to Kingsville.   no passengers was hurt but I had the Coldest Ride up that night I Ever had I think.   no fire   all the passengers in one Box Car.   it was very well for you not being a board   we had a ruff time of it.   well as regardes business I can only Say they are a Good lot of negros in market here for Sale but to Say they will be Sold I cannot.   the presumtion is they will be Some Sold any how. therefore you will please make arrangements for me to Get money here if you please.   I hate very much to come down to Get money on all occasions.   I am not ceartain I will Remain here on monday as I See a Good lot to be Sold in Darlington on monday.   however I will be here on Tuesday any how and I hope you will not fail in Getting the matter arranged.

A. J. McElveen to Z. B. Oakes,
Sumterville, S.C., 6 February 1855. (257)

I haste to drop you a line   I wrote yesterday intending to Sending by Benbow   he left the letter at the hotel nothing Sold worth buying yesterday.   I will Send down the Girl which I have bin talking So much a bout.   you will please Keep her pretty close and let no one See her from Sumter   the old lady & man Says I must Sell her any how and pay for her when I Get her Sent off.   they say they must have $600 for her.   I hope you may be able to Get her off this week as men may be in town for that Purpose attending the Races.   I think I will be in Georgetown on monday next as a Sale of negros takes place there on that day.   please write me to Georgetown   the conditions of Sale is one third cash and if I buy I will come over to make arrangements.   I will leave here on Thursday, and 1 think I will be over nex week from Georgetown   I dont See any thing offring here worth attention   do write me over to Georgetown   Moses

---

cashed the draft   I heard no further of Geting money   I hope it is all arranged by this time as you Stated

A. J. McElveen to Z. B. Oakes,
Sumterville, S.C., 7 February 1855. (256)

in adition to my letter yester I have failed in Sending the Girl down.   I could not Send her from the fact I would bin liable to be bailed   therefore I am done with property where they are no title.   I leave here tomorrow for the low Country and perhaps I will Pick up Something on my way. you need not write to Georgetown as I Give out Going down. I want to prepare for a Sale that will take place in Camden on the first monday in March.   one hundred negros to be Sold   Mr W. M. Green Says try and Sell his old woman for $375.   if you cant Get that he wants to take her back   you will please write him to Bishopville and oblige me   please let me hear from you on Recept of this. Should I buy any thing down the country that is as far down as I go I will come on down   I must Pay Mr Gordon in my Rout So if I dont buy I will be here in a few days

A. J. McElveen to Z. B. Oakes,
Sumterville, S.C., 24 February 1855. (242)

nothing of importance Since I left you.   on my way up I met the boy Calep who was Sold to Mr Whaley.   he is in Kingstree Jail and has bin there for Some time   if Mr Whaley will autherise me I will take him out, and Send him to you.   I Suppose the Expences are Some fifteen or twenty Dollars.   the boy has bin advertised in the papers for two months, I was informed.   I cannot attend to it before after Sale day   perhaps you Cannot Get the order before that time.   howerver I will do it as Soon as posible.   let me Know Somthing about the reward, and if the Girl patience has bin Seen Since they Runaway.   what did Mclaw do with his too boys   they will be Sold on the 7th March 26 negros 30 miles from this place   assigned negros.   they are offred at private Sale   the likely Runaway boy was looking after me in my absence   I hope I will be able to Get him Soon I look for him tonight   you will please Send up Mr Greens old woman to Sumterville as he wants her home.   also Send me bill of Expences   the Runaway fellow belongs to Mr Greens Brother.   dont Say any thing about the fellow as I in tend to Get a bargain if I Can   let me here from you as Early as posible as I will be absent the last of next week

A. J. McElveen to Z. B. Oakes,
Sumterville, S.C., 26 February 1855. (238)

Mr Green is very anxious for his negro woman Sent up I would be Glad if you would Send her up immediately.   the boy is in Jail which I thought of Geting.   he was taken by the dogs.   the Major Says he will not take less than $900. he Says I must Send him to you but not Send him a lone   I will Send him if I can meet any body Going down   other wise, he Says I must not Send him   [he?] is fearful the boy will make his escape.   do Send the woman & bill of Expences, and I will attend to it   it is So cold I cant hardely write.   we had a Snow last night   let me Know how the negro market continues.   Greens boy will bring a bout $850, from the Former prices   the boy must not be Sold in the State that is to Remain here.   Send Whaleys order for Calep   he is in Kingstree Jail   what can I Give for likely fellows, plow Boys   Girls, what is Girl 11 worth   tolerable likely

A. J. McElveen to Z. B. Oakes,
Sumterville, S.C., 28 February 1855. (234)

I drop you a line by Mr Green, in answer to yours this Evening.   Mr Green is brother of the Major who I bought the Girl from Clar, also the owner of the boy, which I wish you to do the best you can for him   the title is unquestionable   you will please deliver Mr G the old woman, &c   I looked at a woman to day but did not buy her   they ask $150 more than I could Give   you will please write me to Camden as I will be there on monday ceartaine   I See no chance to buy here.   I think I will leave the market until it Gets better.   I have just heard from Mr Briscoe   times are hard in Mississisipi   I will draw Some money to morrow I would like you to write me by Green   I Remain well

A. J. McElveen to Z. B. Oakes,
Sumterville, S.C., 2 March 1855. (230)

I was offred a prety likely Girl to day   a molatto   18 years old   Said to be a Good Seamstress   She was bought by Mr How formely of charleston   She is bin Raised By the Miss [Hendrix?] of darlington and was owned in charleston by Mad Salvow[88]   She is a bout the Sise of [Gilchrest?] Beck Good teeth   talks well   Strate hair & they want $950. what is She worth in the market   She has a mother in charleston and wants to Get back.   I offred $800 and thought that Enough.   you will write me to Camden and Give me your Idies as I leave here tomorrow and will not be here nom[ ] before I See the parties.   they are to Meet me at withersp[oon?] Sale on the 7th.   Can you be up to Cam-

---

88. French-born F. Madame Salvo operated a dry goods business on King Street near Spring Street in Charleston. Charleston city directory (1855), 93; U.S. Census, 1860, S.C., Charleston, 501.

___

den as I have men to Hand my Security.   I would like to be
Recommended by you   if you cannot come up [Send?] a
few wordes to the comissioner in Equty as the Sale is in his
hands.   I dont Know that I will buy.   that [depends?] on
prices.   dont faget to Say what you think about the price
of the Girl.   I [think?] this is a very Good Girl and [well?]
behaved as far as I Saw   [Mr?] how wants to Sell me two
others   I did not See them

A. J. McElveen to Z. B. Oakes,
Camden, S.C., 5 March 1855. (226)

        yours was duly Recd'   I cant Say anything of intrust
the Sales closed, and the hiest prices I Ever Saw   they aver-
aging a bout Seven hundred Dollars   I leave here in the morning and will be at a nother Sale on wednesday   I Suppose
I will have Some chance as the Sale will be for cash, that is
if the creditors do not come in competition.   let me here
from you on Recept of this.   if I cannot buy in the country
at prices to Suite what will I do.   come down and lay over,
I recon.   the negros Sold from $50 to 1500.   young
women Sold as high as $1200, but few likely fellow Single.
the most of the fellow was in famleys.   Boys from 15 to 17
Sold from $900 to $1100.   you See they was no chance for
me.   the 98 negros Sold for a bout $70,000.

A. J. McElveen to Z. B. Oakes,
Sumterville, S.C., 8 March 1855. (224)

        yours came to hand this afternoon.   I have nothiing to
write of intrust.   I was at the Sale yesterday.   the Gang
of negros was very ordenary   consequentely I did not buy.
I would be Glad if you would Get an order from Mr Whaley, if
he wish me to bring his boy down.   after I Get the order it

will take me two or three days to Get him here as the distance are at least 45 miles   I dont See any chance to buy.   it is Posible I may meet with chances but it is unceartain   however I will be ready when they offer   I would as Soon be there lofing as here   I will write to white immediately & also to Brown.   I wrote from charleston to White to Send the boy to Mr Brown.   I have not heard from Either   Since I am compeled to draw Some money on Saturday I have bin putting it off hoping to make Some purcheses

I hope this will meet you all well as it leaves me.

H. Elijah McElveen to Z. B. Oakes,
Sumterville, S.C., 7 July 1856. (651)

owing to my Ill health during the last Spring I was not able to take down any negroes during that time but as my health has Somewhat improved I can attend to business of that kind if I knew what the price of negroes were.   therefore I wish Some information from you.   I know of a Girl 16 years old but cross Eyed   likely otherways   I would like to know what I can afford to give for Such   also a likely young woman with her first child (young) and yellow.   what can I afford to give for that lot.   pleas let me know Immediately, Say in three days.   let your address be to Shiloah, Sumter District, S.C and I remain yours Truly

A. J. McElveen to Z. B. Oakes,
Sumter, S.C., 8 July 1856. (642)[89]

yours was duly Reced, yesterday.   I have Just arrived from Darlington.   the Sale was over before I arrived in con-

---

89. Sumterville was renamed Sumter in 1855.

sequence of the train laying over for company orders was Isued for the first time for the train to lay over and I took it on foot for ten miles & did not Get there in time   therefore you See it was not my fault.   however I dont think they was any Bargains   only one fellow Sold a bout thirty for $1000. the ballance famleys, at pretty high figurs.   a few will be offred me to day.   Some I wrote you a bout.   I think they are no chance to buy them under the figurs I gave.   I will try.   negros is very high.   I Saw Col weatherly of molborough Dist.   he is wanting to buy & wants to come to charleston   he told me he heard the yellow fever had broke out there   do let me Know, if it is the case, and if So all the negros comes in market Buy them, and if the fever continues Send the negros up to me   I Can Sell in Co-lumbia or Even here much higher than in charleston   I See a new trader in here from N.C.   Mr Watson.   he told me he paid $1800 dollars for two Boy not Groon in Columbia last week.   {write me Soon   all up yet.}   Mr Oakes as Regards the two negros McElveen Sold to wilson, I never new the negros was for Sale.   I dont live So far from town. they could wrote me very Easely.   I Send to the Postal once a week when I dont Go myself   you Recolect I could not buy three negros from the two McElveens Early in the Spring I was down and told you the prices and you Said it was two high   I Supposed they did not like it and Give me no chance. you can See from this the reason.   as regards the Boy Tom who you Sold to Mr Eason[90] I think he is out of my Reach, as I bought him Some 6 miles below this place   I Received

---

90. Perhaps George W. Eason, clerk, 26 Vendue Range, Charleston. In 1855 Charleston auctioneers Alex. Calder, H. Cobia and Company, and C. H. West listed 26 Vendue Range as their place of business. Charleston city directory (1855), 33, 121.

letter from him concerning the boy.   do Say to them, I will [in for]⁹¹ the Parties, have him taken if Posible

A. J. McElveen to Z. B. Oakes,
Sumter Court House, S.C., 10 July 1856. (645)

this will inform you our Baby was Born last night half past 11 oclock   the finest Boy you Ever Saw   I think he would weigh at least 10 lbs.   he is double fisted chap they are all doing as well this morning as can be Expected.   Give our love to all your famly and tell Mrs O if we live and nothing happens to prevent I will bring them down to See you all.

I offred Richardson $1350 for his two negros.   he Refused to take it.   the fellow is Rather light   he weighs 121 lbs, but Good teeth & not whiped   the little Girl he was offrd $475   I thought the boy worth a bout $850 and at that price they would not Sell for cost but I Supposed the fellow would Bring $9 to $950 &c and the little Girl 500 at best.   I will See him on Saturday and I may Get them   if I do I will Send them down, on monday.   I dont think they are much diferance in Richardson two negros & McElveens the negros of McElveens may be a Shade likely but not more. do let me here from you on Recept of this.

A. J. McElveen to Z. B. Oakes,
Sumter, S.C., 28 July 1856. (648)

your two letters came Safe to hand this day   I cannot amegin what little negros are offring here   I have not heard of any, only three of one of my neighbours and he ask $1500

---

91. [in for] is probably "inform."

for them   all girls   one a bout 12 & 10 & 5.   I will
have the Refusal of them, Soon   I thought $1200 was all
they was worth   I am Called on to look at a famly of
negros in Darlington which I will attend to on next Thursday.   do let me here from you often   we are all Getting
on pretty well   the Boy is well Except the [thrash?].[92]   I
have Suffred for Rain very much   I am Glad to hear from
the family

A. J. McElveen to Z. B. Oakes,
Sumter Court House, S.C., 2 August 1856. (629)

I have bin out two days.   Stock is not plenty   however a few was offred me at high figures.   I met with one
man   he Speaks of Selling one to three fellows   one I
Saw no. 1   nothing less than one thousand can buy Such
fellows here.   weighs a bout 165 to 170   I did not weigh
him but I am prety Good in Guessing.   I Stood by the
boy   he is one and half inch lower than I am   he is a
bout 22 years of age   the old man is to let me Know as
Soon as he Sees his Son   he Give the fellow to his Son
and he will not Stay with him.   I cannot buy Such fellow
here for less than $1000   let me hear from you as regards
the matter   one cook 35   one field hand 25   offred
woman at $1200.   I offred $650 for the field hand   the
cook I thought a bout 400 to 450   they are not very prime,
what may be called ordanary   I did not wish to buy unless
prime   I think I will Get a chance at the three little negroes
you wrote me about   the fact is this, the negros could not
be Bought for the Sums you ment[iond?]   the infermation
you Got could not be Relied on.   however, Such might bin

---

92. [thrash] is probably thrush, a throat and mouth disease caused by a
fungus. It occurs especially in young children.

the case the man who has [the?] matter in hand at present might [told?] your informent   he Supposed Such Sums could buy Such aged negros but he tells me the owner as I hapen to meet with him on my Rout, he was under promise to Give the western trader the Refusal.   I am to See Mr Bradford[93] to day, the present owner of the three little negres, and if we trade at all we cannot close before monday.   do let here from you as regards the cook & field hand, women the persons wish very much to Sell them   I was told by Good authority they was two millions Dollars in Richmond to buy negros.   I have not bin home for three days   I left them all well.

A. J. McElveen to Z. B. Oakes,
Sumter, S.C., 8 August 1856. (630)

I am Sory you will not answer my letters.   I hope you will Excuse me troubling you So much.   I cannot Get a long well without Getting advice.   negros offring me at high prices and I must here from the market, or I am at a lost to make high offers.   therefore I hope you will Give me advices in Every letter.   I am aware you are at a lost to Give advices from discrption but what can I do unless I Get them often.   I will Give you Some names and ages and do let me here from you immediately, as the parties will Sell Sooner or later.   Girl 11 [5][94]   January 9 [4] or 10.   Eliza 9 [4] or ten   Nancy 7 or 8 [37].   three of the negros are the ones you wrote me a bout   they are all near molaters.   I

---

93. The 1850 census, Sumter District, listed several planters surnamed Bradford. Teel, *1850 Census, Sumter-District*, dws. 704, 1191, 1323, 1771, 1782, 1784, 1916.

94. Numbers in brackets were written in superscript either before or after the preceding number or word indicated.

am ask for the four negros $2000.   I offred $1800.   I have Reasons to believe they cannot be Bought for $1800. I also have a list of 9 more negros.   you will oblige me very much to Say or Send me a price to offer for them   Capt Benbow Says I must Sell them if I cant buy them, and if we cannot trade he wish me to take them out west for him.   you will be Kind Enough to Give me an Estimate   my Estimate is $3200.   Sam 45 [5] very prime and fine waggoner. his wife [5] 45 very ordenary   two Boys the Same Size Capers & Collins 12 [10].   Walby 8 [4]   lesly 6 [3] Liah 3 [2].   two motherless children   moses 4   Binky 3.   the children are all likely, and the father is Stout fellow   will weigh 160 or more   his teeth is not Good nor his wife   do write me on Recept of this.

A. J. McElveen to Z. B. Oakes,
13 August 1856. (632)

yours came Safe to hand.   I am Sory the yellow fever is broke out.   we cannot look for any business before frost. under these con siderations I think I had better Go west.   I will have 7 negros   4 of my own and 3 of the Est.   my fellow is out yet and I dont Know whether I can Get him or not   I have wrote for the Dogs and look for them to day. my boy has bin out three months, I have not whiped him the first time.   I wants to make up a lot of negros by the first of Oct.   a Gentleman in *Ala* have promised to help me Sell if I will come.   he lives below montgomery   he moved from this State, Mr Cook[95] a Settled farmer.   I think I can Depend on him   I have promised to meet him by 10 Oct in montgomery   I want to comence bying by the first of

---

95. T. Cook, Fort Deposit, Alabama. See T. Cook to A. J. McElveen, 21 August 1856, Oakes Papers.

Sept   I want to buy a bout 10.   I think what I Get on commission will pay the Expences.   I can Get Benbows 9, and Mr Lewis[96] has 7.   he promise me those on commission   will pay the Expences on 15 I think.   let me here from you on the Subject if you please.   I heard to day a m[an?] or company wanted to buy 100 negro men in Tallahassee Fla. at tall prices.   we are all tollerable well   little Oakes was not well last night   I left him Sleeping this morning.

T. Cook to A. J. McElveen,
Fort Deposit, Ala., 21 August 1856. (633)

Dr Sir   you will find my hand is So nervous that you will hardly be able to read this Epistle   however your last letter came duly to hand   I have bin still informing myself when occasion [saoted?][97] in relation to your wishes and I find Encouragaement for you   for instence I was in Haynville last monday and I Saw a woman Sold for 30 or 35 years of age that I am Satisfied will not See fortty again for seven hundred cash up and no grumbling and I then made Same move to several in your name and they Expressd a wish to Know when you arive with yrs   well it only remains for me to say come on   you will find a ready market   Now respecting your arrangements is all I need name to you   I can not promise you to meet you in Montgry the 10th of

---

96. Possibly William Lewis, Sumterville planter and Ordinary, Sumter District, who co-owned the Sumter *Banner* with John S. Richardson, Jr.; or W. Lewis, a slave trader. Teel, *1850 Census, Sumter-District*, dw. 1871; Conveyance Files, vol. PP, pp. 69–72, Sumter County Register of Mesne Conveyance; Gregorie, *History of Sumter County*, 455, 517, 537; Tadman, *Speculators and Slaves*, 273.

97. [saoted?] is probably "sooted" or "suited."

Octr.   if I can I will but I would advise you to offer them in Montgry if the signs of the times would autherise and keep my region in reserve   you Know reserve is verry good Sometime   my next duty is to point out how and where you will find me   well Enquire for the Stage road to Mobile and 35 miles below Montgry   Enquire for fort deposite and at fort deposite you will find Mr. Stone merchnt & Mr. Fronabarger Blacksmith that will tell you where to find me only 4 miles and all will be right

ps

if you wish any thing more you must Keep me informd by letter & I will serve you this term

A. J. McElveen to Z. B. Oakes,

Sumter Court House, S.C., 30 August 1856. (640)

yours came Safe to hand few days a go.   I have bin busy Engaged hunting the Boy Joe for ten days.   I cannot find him.   I have the Blood hounds.   we have lot one & Run them hours   he had free pass.   I am fearful I will have hard time to Get him or Considerable trouble to find him   I think he is in Santee Swamp.   I have good many looking out for him.   I want to buy a few negros before I Go to montgomry   however I will come down in Sept if the fever will allow me.   I would like to See you before I leave do Right me a bout the fever if you please as I dont wish to be in any danger.   we have had only one case of fever on the place and very light   do let me hear from the market also.   the Baby — all is well   Excuse this as I am in hurry to take the hounds to R.R.

A. J. McElveen to Z. B. Oakes,
Sumter Court House, S.C., 1 September 1856. (607)

I haste to drop you a line in conclusion to my last   also Enclose you my friends letter, I Received Since I wrote you.[98] I think Mr Cook will do to depend on.   However they may be Great changes in the markets before I could Get these.   I want to Go if nothing happens to prevent me.   I cannot Say they are any ceartainty of Getting negros to Sell on comision.   you Know how people are in the country.   they put off Selling till the last hour Rather than to Sell property to pay there debts, and will often make promises and turn Round and make other arrangements.   well I want Some ten or fifteen negros for the first trip   I think I had better advertise for negros, to buy or Sell on comis.   if I cant Get them on comis, allow me to Give a draft on you at 30 days, payable at the Bank S.W R.R.[99]   let me here from you amediately   I will not make any arrangement with any person before Oct   that will Give me till the first of November to meet the payment

P.S. I will try and come down and See you the last of Sept, if think they are no danger of the fever

---

98. See T. Cook to A. J. McElveen, 21 August 1856, Oakes Papers.
99. The Southwestern Railroad Bank, chartered in 1836, was the financial arm of the Louisville, Cincinnati and Charleston Railroad Company, which subsequently united with the South Carolina Canal and Railroad Company to form the South Carolina Railroad Company. The stock owned by the state in the railroad company and bank helped finance most railroad projects in the state after 1847. Ford, *Origins of Southern Radicalism*, 220 n. 5.

A. J. McElveen to Z. B. Oakes,
Sumter Court House, S.C., 8 September 1856. (608)

Yours came Safe to hand this morning.   I am very Glad to hear of the apprehension of Joe   do take Good Ceare of him   do notice if his leg is well and if not let me Know   I had it nearly well when he left me   I want to Give him one hundred lashes as Soon as I come down as he has no Cause for leaving me   he Runaway from work and nothing Else.   dont believe any thing he tells you.   I will be down in a bout two weeks if nothing happens to prevent.   I Suppose I can Sleep on the Island[100] and be Safe from the fever.   I hope you will try and help me Get a few negros as I am Satisfied money can be made and I hate to Submit to the prices here.   you Recolect the 4 little negros I wrote you offred me at $2000, and you Said $1600 was a bout what they would be worth here from discription.   well a man from Tennessee came on and Give the $2000 for them Mr Oakes these are facts.   if negros can be picked up in Charleston for [1 pr?] cent lower than up here I dont See why we cannot make money.   I am Ready to work in the business and work Right.   they are lot off negros up here offred for Sale   the Owner Mr Lewis told me he was offred $650 Round.   60 in the lot   a bout half fellows.

as Regards Joe you can do as you think best with him I wish to See him.   I Suppose it will be Some time before he will be fit for Sale as he needs feeding up   I have close & Blanket for him   he left them home   what is Joe worth.

myself & famly Respects to you & famly.   the little Baby is doing well.   I think he will Soon talk   Right me on Recept of this.

---

100. Probably Sullivan's Island, "with its cool refreshing breezes" and across the Cooper River from Charleston. Charleston *Daily Courier*, 2 August 1854.

A. J. McElveen to Z. B. Oakes,
Sumter Court House, S.C., 16 September 1856. (615)

I am very Sorry you have not writen tome this week.
I was in hopes you would Satisfied me in regard to Going
west.   I cannot buy any thing here to make money on in
charleston.   I am ceartain I can make money in Ala.   S
N Brown is here and have Bought Some 20 up to this time.
you may look for me down next week   Brown Says he will
Go down with me   do write me immediately   what is
Boy 17 and his mother worth, a bout 40.   Buy Every thing
you can Get that is likely for I tell you negros are in Demand.

I am loosing Ground   ceartin persons Coming in and
Buying Every thing under me.   do let us Spur up once
more   I think it will turn out to our advantage.   Good
fellows are worth $1200 in ala. Ceartain, and young lads Say
15 to 17 are worth $1000.   young women likely are worth
$1000, &c.   I Suppose you are posted in ala markets

A. J. McElveen to Z. B. Oakes,
Sumter Court House, S.C., 4 October 1856. (586)

I haste to drop you a line   I have drawn on you to
day.   I hope you will be Kind Enough to Except.   I have
not Seen any negros that I could buy Since I left charleston
I will try to Get Some on monday but I am affraid to pay high
prices   I hear to day negros are falling in Richmond   one
Girl offred me this Evening for $750   not quite Grown
prety likely   the three little negros I have not Seen those
I discribed to you.   I will be over on Tuesday or wednesday, and call on Bamberd[101]   do write me to that place

---

101. W. S. Bamberg, Bamberg, S.C. See W. S. Bamberg to friend, 2 December
    1856, W. S. Bamberg to Z. B. Oakes, 12 December 1856, Oakes Papers.

---

do try and Get me a few negres if you can and I will come down Thursday, and Get them⠀⠀⠀all well

A. J. McElveen to Z. B. Oakes,
Bamberg, S.C., 10 October 1856. (589)

⠀⠀⠀I haste to drop you a line in answer to yours⠀⠀⠀I meet very little Encuragement this the third day Since I came over. I can make a trade with Bamberg, By taking his note payable in the Bank at 60 days⠀⠀⠀that is the best he can do for me. he offers me prety likely Girl & $800, for one famly⠀⠀⠀the old woman & 3 children 10, 7, 3 years old⠀⠀⠀I think his Girl will bring Readly $900 in ala.⠀⠀⠀I will be down in the morning at 8 oclock.⠀⠀⠀I will leave the negros here⠀⠀⠀I would be Glad you would meet me at the depot, and try and have the negros up at the depot, So as to leave on 10 oclock train. I would Rather take the 4 oclock train in the afternoon if you think they are no dangers to lay over.⠀⠀⠀I am affraid of the fever⠀⠀⠀meet me any how if you can and if you cant Get the negres Ready, I Suppose they will not be much danger to be in the city 8 hours in the day.

A. J. McElveen to Z. B. Oakes,
Bamberg, S.C., 15 October 1856. (593)[102]

⠀⠀⠀I Enclose you Bambergs note, for Six fifty ($650)⠀⠀⠀that is the Best he could do for me.⠀⠀⠀he also wish you to inform him the Bank you (leave it in) or place it in.⠀⠀⠀I leave here

---

102. Written in ink on back of letter:

[Dito?]___	24	[Dit?]___	17
[Dt?]___	30	[t?]___	30
[D?]___	6	[t?]___	13
	0		0

on 11 oclock train.   all the negros are well at present   I
will write you in a day or too after I arrive in Montgomery.
I made no trade Since I left you.   I might make Some trades
to day, but I cant lay over no longer

A. J. McElveen to Z. B. Oakes,
Montgomery, Ala., 15 October 1856. (596)

I arrived here on yesterday Evening.   I find trade not
very Brisk and not much Stock in market, and I dont here of
much coming through.   the trade is not farely opened.
a few negros are Selling and at tall prices.   if I was Ceartain
I could Get the prices, I would be willing to lay over here all
the winter.   the Supposition is negros will be higher.   I
met with a man on the cars yesterday, that is likely to buy the
Seamstress.   I feel Encouraged, but Cant Say it will Remain   I have not bin here long Enough.   I Expect to
take a trip out in the interear, in a day or too.   I will Right
you in a bout week or ten days   Mr Oakes I think it will
pay well, much better than buying and Selling in charleston.   no other but likely negros will Sell that is at tall
prices.   we are all well   I stoped with Brown & Bulger.[103]   if you write me write to the Ceare of Brown &
Bulger

A. J. McElveen to Z. B. Oakes,
Hayneville, Ala., 21 October 1856. (601)

I am here laying over a few days.   I have had Some
offers   I have not Sold any thing up to this time.   the
Carpenter is out on trial for a few days.   the Gentleman

---

103. Probably a Montgomery trading firm. McElveen might also be refer-
     ring to S. N. Brown and the firm of Bulger and DeVane.

will See me on Saturday that will be the 24th, and will decide Dr Weatherly is here   he lives in his tents   he told me he Sold ten negros last week at very fare prices.   he is following the Counties Round attending Courts   Mr Oakes James is cutting up.   his Contrariness.   I could Sell him like hot cakes if he would talk Right.   you may blame me but I tell nothing on him but the fact and Dr Weatherly will tell the Same.   the Boy is trying to make himself *unsound.* he Says he wore a trust in charleston.   I think it would be well to See his former master and Know the facts, and write me to Montgomery.   I will be there next week   also advise Mr Brown the course to persue.

S. N. Brown told me he would garantee any thing I done in the way of trading.   By all means I will Give full warrantee by instructions you Give me So I hope the matter will not amount to much.   I hope this will find you all well

A. J. McElveen to Z. B. Oakes,
Montgomery, Ala., 1 November 1856. (579)

I Enclose you Draft on New york for two Thousand Dollars, the Sale of Patrick & moses, the Best I Could do in the present State of things   I made Some other Sales of my pore Scrubs.   I lost money on them.   the fact is you cannot do much with defective negroes.   Bad teeth & old ones.   I leave in the hands of Mess Rice[104] Burch & Kirkland four negroes namly James William Clearisa & Rody for Sale.   I will advise them for the Best   also you can confer with them.   I paid half pr cent on the Exchange   I Suppose they will be a little lost on the Exchange.   that is the lowest it can be bought here at.   James has promised

---

104. Rice was probably an employee of the Montgomery trading firm of Burch Kirkland and Company.

me to do better.   I will be down to See you the last of this
month or the first of Decr.   I would be Glad you would
Get up lot of Good likely Boys & Girls.   low Country
negros dont take well, these Boys dont take well   I Receivd
your letters two I think to the Ceare of Brown & Bulger, also
one at Haynville.   to Push Sales a man must come down
in prices that is ceartain   politicks Runs So high Keeps
trade Back after the Election   I have no doubt Business will
improve   the fare comes off here the 11 12, 13th   they
look foward for Business to take a change.   Brown tills me
the Doct has Examined James.   I have not Called on him
for a Certificate.   I will not do it yet a while.   James tills
me he left his truss at his wife house, you can ascertain the
facts   I will leave here to day for home.   I will Retain
the Duplicate   if you need it I will Send it down.   Tell
Ms O howdy & children.

A. J. McElveen to Z. B. Oakes,
Sumter, S.C., 4 November 1856. (562)

    I arrived home Safe all well   I Suppose you have Re-
ceivd all communications from montgomery.   I made a Sale
after I wrote you   the Girl Rody, $850 at 60 days intrust
included.   I will Enclose the note to you, and if you are
pushed for money you can draw on the parties.   I Got in
Sumter in time for the Sale yesterday   I Recon that will be
a bout the last of the traders flying Round   we had Some
8 or ten traders in Sumter   Mr Oakes I want to Return to
ala by the first of Decr.   if you can pick up a lot of young
negroes I will take more time and be a ble to Get Better prices.
all the negros Sold yesterday Sold high.   Without Some
miss hap I may be called on to assist Selling a lot of 50 negroes.
the negroes are bought and I think they will not be put in the
market before next month.   if I take the negroes I will let

you Know.   as Regards the negroes I left in montgomery for Sale I Got a Recipt for the Said negroes James William and Clearisa at the following limits   William not to be Sold for less $1375, James for $1400, & Clearisa[105] for $1075.   the house is bound for the a bove prices or Return Said negros or firm Signed Burch Kirkland & Co.   I hope I done what was Right.   I will also Enclose you the Duplicate in the Event of any thing Rong, or delay of Draff from montgomery.

A. J. McElveen to Z. B. Oakes,
Sumter, S.C., 17 November 1856. (573)

This will informe you I have bin very unwell Since I came home and my little Boy has bin very Sick from cold   we are all Getting better for afew dayspast   I am Know wating to Get a lot of negroes if they are any chance to Buy them the chances are prety Bad up here   however I have the promise of one fellow at $900 on the first monday in next month and I am to look at 7 more the last of this week   they are young negroes   our country are never cleare of Buyers I am ceartain if I could Keep a lot of negroes in Sumter I could Sell them well.   we have not bin cleare of one or more traders Since last July.   I would like to Start with a lot the first of Decr, if they are any chance to Get them   do let me here from you on Receipt of this   you may have a letter in the office for me at this time   I have not bin to the office this week   do let me Know if you have heard from the negroes I left in montgomery   {I left your Bills of Sale with

---

105. Although McElveen wanted Oakes to sell Clearisa for $1075, the Mont-gomery firm of Burch Kirkland and Company sold her for $950, minus $42.20 for expenses, including board, taxes and commission. See Burch Kirkland and Company to Z. B. Oakes, 29 November, 14 December 1856, Oakes Papers.

_____

Mr Rice for Said negroes}   {I paid all Expences up to the time I left Except a few days hire, horse and buggy.}

A. J. McElveen to Z. B. Oakes,
Sumter Court House, 20 November 1856. (570)

yours of the 15th came Safe to hand   it is out of my power to Send any funds to you at present.   I beg for indulgence   I cannot Explain matters & things until I See you and one thing ceartain if you cannot indulge me *I am Ruined in business*   I hope you will be Kind Enough to Give me time   I will do my best to Satisfy you   I hope you will not be vexed with me   I am mortified to Know I have not done what I intended to do for you in Sending funds to you do try and Get up Some Stock and let me take another trip if I have not done Right I hope you will pardone me for it this time.   my Respects to all the famly   {I wrote you yesterday not Knowing your letter ha came.}

A. J. McElveen to Z. B. Oakes,
Sumter Court House, S.C., 2 December 1856. (530)

yours came Safe to hand and contents noticed   I am very sory to hear Such news from Montgomery.   I have always tried to do for the best to advance our intrust in business   it appears things will turn out to the Contrary.   as regards the Boy James he was left at the Stable near the office in order to Keep him from being idle, and it was Satisfactory to Burch Kirkland & co   if it was not why did they Give me a Recipt for him   I will inclose it to you to Show you they are bound for the negroes at the limits Specified   the prices of negroes here are Such I dont See any chance to buy to make a dollar and what am I to do   I cant Say the traders west are always here buying Every thing.   I will be down next week and Bring the amount you want from the agent.   I Expect to Get a negro from Doctor Mcoley on commission and I promised to See him before I left   he wanted me to take him west but I Suppose they will be no chance.   as regards the note on [Sanders?] certainly Brown & Bulger will not let it be protested.   I depended on them perticularly to See the matter arranged.   however I will write them fourth with to See it attended to.   I will do my best to Get Stock and Settle up what I am behind with you. they are a Sale to take place the last of this month and I hope to meet with a chance that might pay Something.   I cannot have him before next monday.   it will take me too or three days to See Mcoley.

A. J. McElveen to Z. B. Oakes,
Sumter Court House, S.C., 30 December 1856. (543)

I called on Mr R Cannon[106] and looked at 3 fellows to day   he asked me $1050 for Each   Says he cant take less for them.   the ages 21 20 26   they will weigh a bout 160 Each   prety likely and prety Good teeth   active fellows one rather low but well put up   in fact all is will formed the heights are a bout [5. 6 or 8 inches   one is about 5 4 in.?][107]   what are they worth in charleston market.   I offred $950.   do write me immediately   they will be Good many Sold here on monday.   I will try my best and buy Some on time   let me Know how the market Stands I am fearful Col weatherly will buy Cannons negroes as he is to call and See them on Saturday.   I See Great many will

---

106. Perhaps R. J. Cannon, farmer, Clarendon District. Teel, *1860 Census, Clarendon District*, dw. 513.

107. [5. 6 or 8 inches   one is about 5 4 in.?] is possibly "5 feet 6 or 8 inches one is about 5 feet 4 in."

be Sold in charleston the first of January, by Purcher.[108]   Mr Burgess[109] has not decided a bout his lot

A. J. McElveen to Z. B. Oakes,
Sumter Court House, S.C., 5 January 1857. (505)

I have bought one Girl only to day   the prices are So high I cant buy to make any thing   the credit prices is out of all reason   White Sids is hear and I think he had better hold on a day or too.   the three fellows I will try & See them, and See what can be done, and buy them if posible a Sale will take place at Darlington C H on the 13 inst.   one thousand negroes will be Sold on that day, on time or Cash. I think I had better attend it as is likely I can buy.   as regards burgesses negroes, they are three or four men trying to buy them   I am Going to See burgesses negroes to-morrow.   Jim Says Look for him Friday or Saturday.

A. J. McElveen to Z. B. Oakes,
Florence, Darlington District, S.C., 7 January 1857. (499)

I have purchesed two fellows this morning from Mr Cannon for $2025.   the best I could do.   they are Good-many offring in this Dist for Sale at high prices   we have the promise of two boys on Friday   Whiteside will be down on Saturday.   I want to attend the Sale over here on the 13th if I can.   Mr Cannon Says he is willing to buy with me and make the papers.   the terms are one third cash and on two years for the ballance.   I must Raise money if posible, or I will be Ruined in Business.   if they are any

---

108. Possibly P. J. Porcher, Charleston broker and auctioneer, 25 Broad Street. Charleston city directories, (1855) 121, (1859) 234.
109. Probably Samuel A. Burgess.

chance to Buy in charleston one time I would be Glad to come in if poseble   do write me on Receipt of this.   I done my best at the credit Sale the other day, but I Saw no chance Jim was present and Saw Every thing pass off.

A. J. McElveen to Z. B. Oakes,
Sumter Court House, S.C., 9 January 1857. (512)[110]

I haste to drop you a line hoping the three negroes will Reach Safe & Jim also.   you will See the market is high up here.   I wish you would Write me as Soon as James arrives.   I want to Know how to manage a bout money if I buy at Darlington C.H.   I think it may pay to attend the Sale over there on the 14 inst if I had a letter to the agent at Darlington C.H.   it might assist me in Giving Satisfaction till I can Get the money   do write me the hiest figures I can pay for prime fellows and Girls Boys &c   if the negroes pays in charleston market, I think they may be better chance to buy here after this if the Demand holds up.

A. J. McElveen to Z. B. Oakes,
Sumter Court House, S.C., 6 February 1857. (498)

I bought three negroes on monday and have failed in Giving Surity So far but hope to do it Soon   the negroes Sold very high   the parties are very purticular in taking Bonds I have not had fare oppertunity as my family has bin very unwell all this week.   I Suppose you heard from the Sale as I Saw T N Gadson[111] up   I did not Speake to him.   as

---

110. Back of letter indicates that McElveen sent it to Oakes by way of Jim White-side. Written in pencil sideways on top of back of letter is "1 Box [cty?]."

111. Thomas N. Gadsden, Charleston broker and auctioneer, State Street, corner Chalmers Street. See Charleston city directory (1859), 234.

---

regards mechanic they was not one worth buying that I
Saw.   they flater the negroes very much in the advertisement   they use Some thirty or forty head to Sell nex Sale
day of the Same lot   the mesles [prevented?] them from
being Sold   what will I do if I fail in Geting the negroes
they will be Sold at my Risk and I am fearful that will blow
me up   I hate very much to pay cash at credit prices.
prehaps I can Get them by paying half Cash.   I dont
See any money in them   one fellow By & woman $2175.
they are two that is the fellow & Boy, will Sell Readely at
high prices   the woman is not very likely.   I hope you
will advise me

I have the promise of one man named to day.   two
men promised to Sine with me on day of Sale and then backed
out   I did not Know one of them was very much in debt,
and he was more Excusable than the other.   one finely
deceived me   one promised me to day I think will Stick
and I have one more to hunt out   I will try very hard and
Get the negroes down next week, if I can.   I will Send you
list of one lot that was offred me to day.   if not Sold will
leave for ala on next wednesday.

woman	Ages	34	
woman	"	26	the Seven negroes can
woman	"	18	be Bought at for $6000.
Girl	"	16	I believe that is the
Girl	"	10	lowest that can buy
Boy	"	13	them here.
Boy	"	14	if you can come up
			the first monday in
			march, I think we

can do Something.   try and come if you can.   I believe
they was Some ten western traders here   a Good many
Bough and paid Cash   negro men Sold here the premest

—————

$1290.   I Saw Owens[112] bid one off at that and a likely Girl
$1140.   you can Judge from that

A. J. McElveen to Z. B. Oakes,
Sumter Court House, S.C., 21 February 1857. (482)

yours was duly Received to day.   I am Sory to Say I
am unable to make arrangements for the negroes.   I am
astonished to think how I am deceived by men who promised
to Give me there names on the Bonds and have backed out.
however, I think of coming down the last of nex week and tell
you all a bout the matter.   I am ceartain the Comissioner[113]
will be as lenitive as he can with me.   I want your advice,
and I would prefere Seeing you.   I will only be down one
day and I hope you will be willing to advise for the best as
you are more Experienced than I am   I am troubled very
much a bout this matter for this Reason I have never failed
before.

A. J. McElveen to Z. B. Oakes,
Sumter Court House, S.C., 2 March 1857. (476)

This will informe you I Got off the negroes I first Bid
off   Mr Chandler took them.   I bid off 4 others which
two of the Chandlers Sined with me.   I have Seven in all
which I will Send down on wednesday morning.   I drawn
on you for $2100 to pay the Amounts which two of the men

—————

112. Possibly R. M. Owings and Company, Hamburg, S.C. See Calendar
and Index, Oakes Papers; Tadman, *Speculators and Slaves,* 126.
113. Probably W. F. B. Haynsworth, Commissioner-in-Equity, Sumter District. Conveyance Files, vol. P, pp. 390–91, Sumter County Register of
Mesne Conveyance. The family name Haynsworth was also spelled
Haynseworth and Haynesworth.

wanted at present also one tenth cash.   I am only interested in the 4 last was bought to day, which consist of man his wife & two children   cost $2580.   the other three will be Sold on Mr Chandlers act, man Boy old woman.   I will Send a letter with the negroes, Giving Some other particulars.   I am So cold I cant hardly write   do Send to the Rail Road on wednesday, at 2 oclock.

A. J. McElveen to Z. B. Oakes,
Sumter Court House, S.C., 4 March 1857. (474)

I Send you 7 negroes which I hope will reach you Safe, and I hope you will do better with them than I Expect.   I am fear ful the negroes will not Sell for cost.   however the negroes are all Sound & healthy and not a bused.   I am only bound for 4 to wit Carter Harriet Powel & Emly   the other three Smart Mary and Simon [belonged?] to Mr Joseph Chandler   I am Eaqually Bound with Mr James R Chandler and Mr R A Chandler in the Sum of $2580.   the first Purchase Mr Joseph Chandler taken and I paid him over $1436.25 — fourteen hundred thirty Six Twenty five cts   please charge Joseph Chandler $1436.25   The amount includs the Expences on three negroes mary Simon Smart for Joseph Chandler   you are autherised to Sign titles for him   Mr James R & Mr R. A. Chandlers will Sign titles with me for the 4 negroes Carter Harriet Powell & Emly.   I paid out for the tenth cash on the hole   also paid to Mr R A Chandler the Sum of $300.   the Blance I paid for Jail fees & the Cash payment &c   I hope you will not misunderstand my Statement   let me hear from you on Recipt of this   I hope you will do all you can for us   the Mr Chandlers are very fine men and better friends of mine than others I depended on up here   their titles are unquestionable, not withstanding the mortgages &c net worth

notice.   if I can do better with the negroes in other markets please let me Know

A. J. McElveen to Z. B. Oakes,
Sumter Court House, S.C., 7 March 1857. (464)

yours was duly Recd.   I hope you will be able to Get
cost for the negroes   do let me hear from you often   will
you be Kind Enough to Give me advice   I have only one
fortnight that is two weeks of Grace on my note   must I
Suffer to be Sued or not.   help me if you can, or I am fearful I will be So far be hind I cant Get up a Gain.

A. J. McElveen to Z. B. Oakes,
Sumter Court House, S.C., 16 March 1857. (462)

I wrote you last weeke hoping to hear from you   will
you be Kind Enough to drop me a line and let me Know what
you think I had best do.   I have only one week of Grace
I hate very much to be Sued   do write me on Recept of this
and oblige yours &c.   perhaps your letter is on the way.
I Sent to the office on yesterday.   I Recevid no letter.   do
let me hear from the negroes.

A. J. McElveen to Z. B. Oakes,
Sumter Court House, S.C., 22 March 1857. (460)

yours came Safe to hand and contents noticed.   I am
very Sorry indeed   I am unable to Get through my dificulties and I am more than Sory you cant help me.   I am
Sued certain   the result I cant Say.   it appears I have no
Encuragement that is my feelings is Such I cannot Express
them   it appears to me I had better Give up all together
and when the parties is ready Go in Jail   however you can

---

better advise me perhaps   I hope you will be willing to Give it.   I Enclose the Bills of Sale to you.   Mr Joseph Chandler Signed too as he Supposed you would Sell the fellow Single.   Mr J. R. Chandler signed one that is for the famly. the other Mr Chandler lived So far I could not See him immediately.   the others are all Suficient   I Suppose it did not matter a bout my Signing   Mr Chandler Request me to Say to you Sell as Soon as posible   dont loose if you can help it   if Posible Get Cost.   I hope you did not misunder Stand me   I have only one third intrust in the famly. Mr Chandler wish account Sales when you Sell.   let me hear from you on Recipt of this.

A. J. McElveen to Z. B. Oakes,
Sumter Court House, S.C., 28 March 1857. (447)

I am Sory you have not wrote me this week.   Mr Chandler wish me to pay over Some money.   I dont wish to draw on you without letting you Know.   they are hard up as well as myself   do let me hear from you as Soon as you Get this.   advise me the course I had better Pursue in my dificulties.   our Court Sits here on the 6th april   that is monday week.   those men are in want of Some money by that time.   do let me hear from you by wednesday as I will be here to meet them on Thursday

A. J. McElveen to Z. B. Oakes,
Sumter Court House, S.C., 29 March 1857. (454)

I haste to drop you a line not noticing the advertisement yesterday.   I wish to lay the matter before you.   a Sale of thirty negroes will take place on the 3 & 4 April.   terms one & two years.   I wish to attend the Sale.   I want you to inform me how the prices of negroes are Ranging at present.   I will buy if I can at Credit or Cash.   please Give me the prices according to qualities.   write me by Return male   I will be at the office on thursday that is on the 2nd april   I will leave home on that day to attend the Sale. it takes place Some 25 miles below me.

A. J. McElveen to Z. B. Oakes,
Sumter Court House, S.C., 4 April 1857. (444)

. your last letter came Safe to hand.   it was too late. I did not attend the Sale   you Give me no infermation a bout Buying and consequently I was at a lost.   I hope I will be better posted up here after   I will not Give up trying. your letter came Safe with Draft one Thousand Dollars   I Receed it on the 2nd inst.   you will please Send Mr Joseph Chandler act Sale of the old woman & two Boys, also the famly to Mr James R Chandler   Send Boath to me.   I am very Sory the famly Sold less than cost   I believe you done the best you could.   deduct one third of the proceeds of the famly and Send the other two and oblige   {I may have chance to buy nex week at Court   let me here from you.}
     P.S. Send one check for Boath Parties.

A. J. McElveen to Z. B. Oakes,
Sumter Court House, S.C., 9 April 1857. (430)

     I am offred a lot of negroes.   I will discribe them as they was discribed to me.   I Expect to see them nex week I have the promise.

Fellow	38	his leg has bin broke & see as well
his wife	37	Sound in Every Respect
Girl	13	All right
Boy	9	" "

Girl   7   "   "

Girl   3   "   "

The negroes are Reppresented to me very likely, with the defect of the fellow   I can tell better when I see them   they ask me $3200 for the 6 negroes   Let me Know what you think they are worth

A. J. McElveen to Z. B. Oakes,

Sumter Court House, S.C., 18 April 1857. (445)[114]

I am very Sory you have not wrote to me.   I have wrote the Second time and no answer   if you have not Recd my two last letters please let me know.   one in relation to the act Sales of the negroes.   the other in relation to the price of a lot of negroes offred me.   prehaps you Send the act Sales to the Mr Chandlers, through a mistake. however that dont make any difference.   I have made my returns to them Satisfactory up to the time I last heard from you   I would like to continue until we Got through   will you be kind Enough to Say any thing a bout the present prices of negroes

---

114. Written on back of letter in ink:

    550

      2-½

    1100

     275

    1375

W. H. McElveen to Z. B. Oakes,
Sandy Grove, S.C., 20 April 1857. (435)

I hear that you have offered a reward of one hundred Dollars for *Solomon*[115] formally belonging to Mr S. A. Burgess and now Runaway and in this neighborhood, it is said. I wish to Know if it is So and where to be delivered whether in Kingstree Jail or charleston   please inform me and oblige
direct to Sandy Grove PO
So. Ca.

A. J. McElveen to Z. B. Oakes,
Sumter Court House, S.C., 22 April 1857. (437)[116]

yours came Safe to hand and act Sales of negroes and draft also.   I will make my return to the Mr Chandler in a few days.   they are a lot of negroes to be Sold here on Sale day in may for Cash   Some 23 head   how is Good likely negroes Selling.   can I buy.   if they are any chance to make any thing you will please advise me immediately.

---

115. Purchased from Samuel A. Burgess, Solomon was sold by Oakes around January 1856 to George A. Savage of Bluffton in Beaufort District. That fall he escaped, heading back to Sumter District. Learning this, Savage authorized Oakes in January 1857 to advertise a fifty-dollar reward for Solomon's apprehension and to sell him as soon as he was taken. But the slave hunters with their dogs had to wait until spring when the waters would fall, making accessible the swamps where Solomon was hiding. G. A. Savage to Z. B. Oakes, 3 January 1857, E. Epps to Z. B. Oakes, 6 March 1857, Oakes Papers.
116. "[Ans?] 24" is written on bottom left corner of letter.

Epilogue: A Highlight of the Sources

With an emerging capitalism, Northern bankers and Charleston slave brokers found themselves in an extended financial network. Victim of the Panic of 1837, New York businessman Lewis Tappan founded in 1841 the Mercantile Agency, which later became known as the R.G. Dun & Co. Local correspondents prepared credit reports and sent them to the home office. In 1962 Dun & Bradstreet Co. deposited 2,580 volumes of these reports, organized by state, at Baker Library, Graduate School of Business Administration, Harvard University. Ironically, Tappan, an abolitionist, provided historians a valuable insight into the business and personal life of Charleston's slave brokers. Another revealing source is the Frederic Bancroft Papers at the Rare Book and Manuscript Library, Columbia University. In preparing *Slave-Trading in the Old South*, Bancroft corresponded with the descendants of planters and slave brokers, including the son of J. S. Riggs. Bancroft visited Charleston several times, and his "Diaries of Southern Trips" contain interesting interviews with local people.[1]

The Sumter-Williamsburg region has produced several local histories rich in detail and folklore. William Boddie's *History of Williamsburg* introduced me to the Scotch-Irish ethnicity of the area. Local women have dominated the writing of Sumter County histories: Anne King Gregorie's *History of Sumter County*, Cassie Nicholes's two-volume *Historical Sketches of Sumter County*, and Janie Revill's *Sumter District*. John Poindexter did a photographic chronicle of Sumter County, 1845–1955. A source of folklore is *Names in South Carolina*, which

enlightened me on the origins of the phrase "Pudding Swamp."
I. E. Lowery's *Life on the Old Plantation in Ante-bellum Days*
is a slave's account of Pudding Swamp and its inhabitants.

Since so much of local history is personal, genealogy is important. Sumter County is blessed with dedicated genealogists. The late Margaret R. McElveen may be considered one of the pioneers. Besides investigating "The Ancestry and Children of John Frierson of Shiloh, S.C.," she studied the Bible Records of the R. L. McElveen family, which are in the collections of the Sumter County Genealogical Society. W. Esmonde Howell, first vice president of that society, is carrying on her work. He became involved by participating in cemetery field work to record the data on tombstones. Genealogists have also produced newsletters, such as the *Sumter Black River Watchman*, and other significant publications. Dorothy Teel, in conjunction with the Three Rivers Historical Society, compiled the federal census returns for Sumter District (1850 and 1860), and Clarendon District (1860). For Sumter District, she included the maiden names of some married women and other pertinent local information.[2]

The South Carolina Department of Archives and History has most of the Sumter County wills, deeds, and master-in-equity files on microfilm, but I found it more helpful to do most of my research at the Sumter County Court House, where I was assisted by Harry Johnson, Register of Mesne Conveyance. Johnson is part of a new breed of state and county officials who are acutely aware of the importance to historians of preserving documents.

My account of A. J. McElveen has been put together with tantalizing bits and pieces which lead to more questions than answers. Newspapers document that McElveen remained a slave trader well into the war years. The Compiled Service Records of Confederate Soldiers show him enlisting in the state militia in 1863 after the Confederate government extended the draft age to over forty. McElveen was stationed at a Confederate military prison in Florence, South Carolina. Yankee prisoners at that notorious camp were offered their freedom if they would join the Rebel cause. What was McElveen's reaction to these "Galvanized Confederates" or to his own situation? How deep was his commitment to the cause? What factors contributed to disillusionment? Defeatism? Unspeakable conditions at the military prison? The well-being of family?[3]

After the war, A. J. McElveen appeared in a household in the 1870 federal census, Sumter County, without his wife Frances. Sumter County conveyance records confirmed that he was a small farmer whose economic existence was at best marginal. What was it like for this former slave trader to compete with freedmen? Was he grateful for the loan he received from a white Republican officeholder, who charged him 25 percent interest, or did he consider himself exploited? Was he a Republican? Did he sympathize with the Ku Klux Klan? What impact did state and local taxes have on his farming operations? R.G. Dun & Co. reported that he died a year after the Panic of 1873.

A. J. McElveen was one of thousands of returning Confederate veterans trying desperately to put their lives back together. Unfortunately, their experiences are seldom examined in histories of the period. This is especially so for those who owned no slaves. They left little behind to document their existences. The McElveen letters give some insight into their aspirations and struggles. Victims of a plantation slavery that reduced many of them to economically marginal men, some, like McElveen, were lured by the possibility of becoming planters and slaveowners themselves. Ambitious and hardworking in their own way, they pursued a Southern version of the American dream of success. The war shattered that dream. Some found themselves struggling as sharecroppers. In order to understand race relations after the war, it is imperative that we study their situation. A Confederate Veterans Project paralleling the Freedmen Project is in order. Fittingly enough, an investigator for R.G. Dun & Co. presaged one veteran's epitaph, "Broke by the War."[4]

Notes

1. James H. Madison, "The Credit Reports of R.G. Dun & Co. as Historical Sources," *Historical Methods Newsletter* 8 (September 1975): 128–31; Robert W. Lovett, "Nineteenth-Century Credit Information," in *Shoptalk: Papers on Historical Business and Commercial Records of New England,* 47–51.
2. These three compilations may be purchased from Three Rivers Historical Society, Hemingway, S.C.
3. G. Wayne King, *Rise Up So Early: A History of Florence County, South Carolina* (Spartanburg, S.C.: Reprint Co., 1981), 49–55; D. Alexander Brown, *The Galvanized Yankees* (Urbana: University of Illinois Press, 1963); James Newton Miller, *The Story of Andersonville and Florence* (Des Moines, Iowa: Welch, printer, 1900). For Sumter newspapers, see South Caroliniana Library, University of South Carolina.
4. Two books which deal with the adjustment of white South Carolinian veterans and their families are Orville Vernon Burton, *In My Father's House Are Many Mansions: Family and Community in Edgefield, South Carolina* (Chapel Hill: University of North Carolina Press, 1985), and Philip N. Racine, ed., *Piedmont Farmer: The Journals of David Golightly Harris 1855–1870* (Knoxville: University of Tennessee Press, 1990). Also see Orville Vernon Burton, "The Effects of the Civil War and Reconstruction on the Coming of Age of Southern Males, Edgefield County, South Carolina," in Walter J. Fraser, Jr., R. Frank Saunders, Jr., and Jon L. Wakelyn, eds., *The Web of Southern Social Relations: Women, Family, and Education* (Athens: University of Georgia Press, 1985), 204–224.